1973

HOW TO UNDERSTAND

WAGNER'S "RING OF THE NIBELUNG."

RICHARD WAGNER.

Frontispiece.

HOW TO UNDERSTAND WAGNER'S RING OF THE NIBELUNG

THE RHINEGOLD (DAS RHEINGOLD)
THE VALKYR (DIE WALKÜRE)
SIEGFRIED (SIEGFRIED)
THE DUSK OF THE GODS (GÖTTER-DÄMMERUNG)

THE STORY AND DESCRIPTIVE ANALYSIS

WITH

MUSICAL EXAMPLES OF THE LEADING MOTIVES OF EACH DRAMA

BY

GUSTAV KOBBÉ

TOGETHER WITH

A SKETCH OF WAGNER'S LIFE

BY

N. KILBURN, *Mus.D.*

LONDON

WILLIAM REEVES, 83 CHARING CROSS ROAD, W.C.

SEVENTH EDITION, REVISED AND ENLARGED.

Printed by The New Temple Press, Norbury Crescent, S.W.

PUBLISHER'S NOTE TO THE SEVENTH EDITION.

THE continuous and increasing demand for this handbook is sufficient testimony to its usefulness to the opera-goer, the music student and to the general public. This seventh edition has been enlarged by the addition of a sketch of Wagner's life, a list of characters and scenes of the dramas. A portrait and facsimile are also given. It is hoped that these additional features will add to its interest and usefulness.

AUTHOR'S PREFACE TO THE FIFTH EDITION.

THE fact that the pamphlet now considerably enlarged which formed the basis of this work passed through four editions shows that it proved useful to the musical public. It made no pretence to be more than a descriptive analysis of the "Ring of the Nibelung," in which the more important leading motives were quoted, so that the reader might identify them and recognise them when he heard them. Care was taken to avoid any technical expressions or discussions. The pamphlet was intended for the general reader.

I have followed the same plan in preparing these articles. In adding considerably to the letterpress —the latter part of the "Siegfried" analysis and the analysis of "The Dusk of the Gods" have been entirely rewritten and the "Notes" converted, with many additions, into the story—and in increasing the number of musical examples, I have simply sought to make the book a little more useful on the same lines.

The success of the work is very gratifying to me, not for personal reasons, but because it affords an indication of a growing interest in the cause in which I wrote.

GUSTAV KOBBÉ.

CONTENTS.

ILLUSTRATIONS.

INDEX TO THE LEADING MOTIVES AS ILLUSTRATED BY THE MUSIC EXAMPLES.

PRONOUNCING INDEX.

Alberich	*Ahl'-beh-reech*
Brünnhilde	*Brün-hil'-deh*
Das Rheingold	*Dahs Rhine'-golt*
Der Ring des Nibelungen	*Dare Ring dehs Nee'-bel-oong-en*
Die Walküre	*Dee Valh'-kü-reh*
Donner	*Dohn'-nare*
Erda	*Air'-da*
Fafner	*Fahf'-nare*
Fasolt	*Fah'-zolt*
Freia	*Fry'-a*
Fricka	*Free'-ka*
Götterdämmerung ...	*Göt-tare-dem'-mer-oong*
Grane	*Grah'-neh*
Gunther	*Goon'-tare*
Gutrune	*Goo-troo'-neh*
Hagen	*Hah'-gen*
Hunding	*Hoon'-ding*
Loge	*Lo'-geh*
Mime	*Mee'-meh*
Siegfried	*Seeg'-freed*
Sieglinde	*Seeg-lin'-deh*
Siegmund	*Seeg'-moond*
Wagner, Wilhelm Richard	*Vahg'-nare, Vil'-helm Ree'-chard*
Waltraute	*Vahl'-trow-teh*

THE RHINEGOLD

(DAS RHEINGOLD)

FIRST PRODUCED IN MUNICH, 1869.

CHARACTERS.		VOICES.
WOTAN	GOD	*Baritone*
DONNER	GOD	*Baritone*
FROH	GOD	*Tenor*
LOGE	GOD	*Tenor*
FRICKA	GODDESS	*Mezzo-Soprano*
FREIA	GODDESS	*Soprano*
ERDA	GODDESS	*Contralto*
ALBERICH	NIBLUNG	*Baritone*
MIME	NIBLUNG	*Tenor*
FASOLT	GIANT	*Baritone*
FAFNER	GIANT	*Bass*
WOGLINDE	RHINE-DAUGHTER	*Soprano*
WELLGUNDE	RHINE-DAUGHTER	*Soprano*
FLOSSHILDE	RHINE-DAUGHTER	*Mezzo-Soprano*
and Niblungs		

SCENES.

Scene 1.	*At the Bottom of the Rhine.*	The Three Rhine-daughters and Alberich.
Scene 2.	*An Open Space on a Mountain Height near the Rhine.*	Wotan, Fricka, Freia, Fasolt and Fafner, Donner, Froh, Loge.
Scene 3.	*The Subterranean Caverns of Nibelungen.*	Alberich and Mime, Wotan and Loge.
Scene 4.	*Open Space on Mountain Heights.*	Alberich, Wotan, Loge; the other Gods and Goddesses, and Erda.

THE VALKYRIE

(DIE WALKÜRE)

FIRST PRODUCED IN MUNICH, 1870.

	CHARACTERS.	VOICES.
SIEGMUND	... VALKYRIE	*Tenor*
HUNDING	... VALKYRIE	*Bass*
WOTAN ...	... GOD	*Baritone*
SIEGLINDE	... VALKYRIE	*Soprano*
BRÜNNHILDE	... VALKYRIE	*Soprano*
FRICKA ...	... GODDESS, WIFE OF WOTAN	*Soprano*
and		
VALKYRIES	... ...	*Soprano and Alto*

SCENES.

ACT I. *The Interior of Hunding's Dwelling.*

PRELUDE AND SCENE 1. Siegmund, Sieglinde.
SCENE 2. Siegmund and Sieglinde, Hunding.
SCENE 3. Siegmund alone, then Sieglinde.

ACT II. *A Wild, Rocky Place.*

PRELUDE AND SCENE 1. Wotan, Brünnhilde, then Fricka.
SCENE 2. Brünnhilde, Wotan.
SCENE 3. Siegmund, Sieglinde.
SCENE 4. Siegmund, Brünnhilde.
SCENE 5. Siegmund and Sieglinde, Hunding, Brünnhilde, Wotan.

ACT III. *On the Top of a Rocky Mountain, Brünnhilde's Rock.*

SCENE 1. The eight Valkyries, Brünnhilde and Sieglinde.
SCENE 2. Wotan, Brünnhilde and the Valkyries.
SCENE 3. Wotan, Brünnhilde.

SIEGFRIED

FIRST PRODUCED IN BAYREUTH, 1876.

CHARACTERS.		VOICES.
SIEGFRIED ...	SON OF SIEGMUND AND SIEGLINDE	*Tenor*
MIME	NIBLUNG	*Tenor*
THE WANDERER	WOTAN IN DISGUISE	*Bass*
ALBERICH ...	NIBLUNG	*Baritone*
FAFNER	GIANT	*Bass*
ERDA	MOTHER OF THE VALKYRIES	*Contralto*
BRÜNNHILDE ...	VALKYRIE	*Soprano*

SCENES.

Act I. *A Cave in a Forest.*

Prelude and Scene 1. Mime, Siegfried.
Scene 2. Mime, The Wanderer.
Scene 3. Mime, Siegfried.

Act II. *Depths of the Forest.*

Prelude and Scene 1. Alberich, The Wanderer (Fafner's Voice).
Scene 2. Siegfried, Mime (Fafner).
Scene 3. Mime and Alberich, Siegfried.

Act III. *Wild Region at the Foot of a Rocky Mountain; afterwards: Summit of the Valkyrie's Rock.*

Scene 1. The Wanderer, Erda.
Scene 2. The Wanderer, Siegfried.
Scene 3. Siegfried, Brünnhilde.

THE DUSK OF THE GODS

(GÖTTERDÄMMERUNG)

FIRST PRODUCED IN BAYREUTH, 1876.

CHARACTERS.		VOICES.
SIEGFRIED ...	SON OF SIEGMUND AND SIEGLINDE	*Tenor*
GUNTHER ...	CHIEF OF THE GIBICHUNGS	*Baritone*
ALBERICH ...	NIBLUNG	*Baritone*
HAGEN	SON OF ALBERICH ..	*Bass*
BRÜNNHILDE ...	VALKYRIE	*Soprano*
GUTRUNE ...	SISTER OF GUNTHER	*Soprano*
THIRD NORN ...	... ...	*Soprano*
WOGLINDE ...	RHINE-DAUGHTER ...	*Soprano*
WALTRAUTE ...	VALKYRIE	*Mezzo-Soprano*
SECOND NORN ...	... ...	*Mezzo-Soprano*
WELLGUNDE ...	RHINE-DAUGHTER ...	*Mezzo-Soprano*
FIRST NORN ...	... ...	*Alto*
FLOSSHILDE ...	RHINE-DAUGHTER ...	*Alto*

Men—*Bass and Tenor.* Women—*Soprano.*

SCENES.

PRELUDE. *On the Valkyrie's Rock.* The Three Norns, Siegfried and Brünnhilde.

ACT I. *The Hall of Gunther's Dwelling on the Rhine. The Valkyrie's Rock.*

SCENE 1. Gunther, Hagen, Gutrune.

SCENE 2. Gunther, Hagen, Gutrune, Siegfried.

SCENE 3. Brünnhilde, Waltraute, Siegfried.

ACT II. *In Front of Gunther's Dwelling.*

SCENE 1. Alberich, Hagen.

SCENE 2. Hagen, Siegfried, Gutrune.

SCENE 3. Hagen, The Men.

SCENE 4. Gunther, Brünnhilde, Siegfried, Gutrune, Hagen, men and women.

SCENE 5. Brünnhilde, Gunther, Hagen.

WAGNER CONDUCTING.

From a contemporary caricature.

To face page 1.

WAGNER

A SKETCH OF HIS LIFE AND WORKS

A LAUREL WREATH AND A HEMPEN ROPE.

IT is said that at a certain club in New York a notice was posted to the effect that members were forbidden to discuss politics, religion and Wagner! For many years in German society it was considered "bad form" to mention Wagner's name, because of the heated disputations which commonly followed. A wealthy Jewish banker in Frankfort, who ardently admired Wagner's music, but as ardently disliked the man, marked his opinions by placing a laurel wreath on the head and a hempen rope round the neck of the great composer's statue which stood in his hall!

Such was the conventional estimate of the man about whom we have to speak; for he was a remarkable man in spite of this, perhaps indeed because of it, for "the greatest mountains cast the deepest shadows."

REFORMER, ESSAYIST AND INSURRECTIONIST.

Richard Wagner is chiefly known as poet, dramatist and musician, but he was many things else. Among others he was a reformer, and reforms we know are not accomplished by civilities. There has to be plain speaking and acting, and both in a literary and a musical sense Wagner indulged in a good deal of this kind of thing, and he thereby made many enemies. But the man has now passed away, and the true value of his life and works is no longer obscured by mere personal feeling and ill-will. Wagner also took a lively interest in human affairs generally, with a sympathy of a wide and, at times, unusual character. For example, a literary essay on which he was engaged two days before his death, and which was never finished, traces the degeneracy of the human race, and our average inferiority to animals in health and beauty, to the violation of the law of love by marriages for rank and money. He also appears to have been ready, so to speak, to back his opinions with characteristically energetic action. This was a man who, though in reality no politician or man of affairs, believing the advancement of his art to be impossible under the unhappy condition of German society, joins the Dresden insurrectionists in 1848 and risks his safety, and even his life, in a futile attempt to alter the social and political situation; whose love for animals leads him to issue burning invectives against vivisection; who does not hesitate to proclaim, and that too at a time when such topics were regarded as dangerous, if not insane, strong views on social reform, religion and art, hydropathy, diet, dress, and the like; views which we now perceive to be of a highly intelligent and even prophetic kind. Such a man can hardly fail to interest even those who are not specially concerned with either music or the drama.

HIS MESSAGE NOT TO THE SUPERFICIAL.

It may, however, be well to say at the outset that to the superficial, Wagner presents but few attractions. No doubt certain of his operas, such as the "Flying Dutchman" and "Lohengrin," have attained a remarkable popularity, but that is because popular taste has advanced, not that these works provide the mere jingle and glitter which usually catches the public ear. Wagner's message is in reality to the earnest souls, to those who have drunk deep of life's experiences. The slow but sure influence of his works testifies to this. Perhaps their rejection and the abuse at first showered upon them is a still stronger testimony, for are we not warned by an ancient and very sacred experience to examine closely and not hastily set aside what is despised and rejected of men? In the high symbolic meaning of it this man "ate his bread with tears." He was acquainted with the wilderness and the solitary place, where only are true messages to be learned. Every now and then there appears among us a special man. Endowed with qualities and capacities out of all keeping with the average of his kind, he is from very necessity misunderstood and, by humanity of the baser sort, reviled and persecuted. His example and work are indeed to such a reproach, and faithful to their low and undeveloped state, they make haste to "stone the prophets." But persecuted men of this kind are often the epoch makers. They are willing to suffer and even to die for an idea. They enfranchise the soul by a life dedicated to the highest human use.

A MUSICIAN OF MYSTIC MEANINGS.

In his peculiar way Wagner belonged to this special order of men, and it is this which entitles him to our attention. Other men have written beautiful music and united it to the drama with noble effect, but not all have drawn their inspiration from so subtle and so spiritual a source. Music such as we find in portions of "Lohengrin," the "Nibelung's Ring" and "Parsifal," defies analysis. It appeals to a higher quality in us than mere intellect and makes us content to rejoice and say with the poet:

> Far better 'tis to bless the sun
> Than reason why he shines.

The music of the mighty Beethoven is distinguished by this same suggestiveness, pervaded as it is by a peculiarly inward and spiritual feeling, a feeling that seems to be in touch with the infinite and which struggles to express in terms of earthly grandeur and beauty even the divine mind itself. We may be quite unable to analyse it, yet rest assured that this sense of ideality and beauty in us, like that of truth in the moral world, will ever remain, to the soul enlightened by sympathy, a sustaining proof of our divine origin and destiny.

HEREDITY.

Richard Wagner was born at Leipzig on May 22, 1813, and died, being a few months off seventy years old, at Venice, on February 13, 1883. He was one of a large family, a thing not altogether to be overlooked, for generally speaking "only" children do not make the most capable men and women. Among musicians, for example, John Sebastian Bach, the greatest the world has yet seen, was one of eight. Wagner's father died when he was quite young, and his mother was afterwards married to Ludwig Geyer, a distinguished actor, who united in himself many artistic qualities. This union brought the boy under influences which gave a distinct tone to his character, and doubtless had much to do with his dramatic tendencies. We do not, however, find in Wagner any marked evidences of heredity. Neither his father nor mother appear to have exhibited in any marked degree artistic qualities, but on this point it is well to be reserved, seeing that what is negative in the parent often appears in positive form in the child, and quiet powers of appreciation and sympathy may be the precursors of even phenomenal talent. Wagner's fitness for the peculiar work he was to do was, however, shown in early life in his attempts at literary composition, for it was not as a musician that his mind began to develop. When he was only eleven years old he projected a grand drama based on Shakespeare, for whom even then he had unbounded admiration, a sort of compound of "Hamlet" and "King Lear." The plan was ludicrously grandiose. Forty odd persons died or were killed in the opening acts, and "in developing the plot," says Wagner, "I found myself compelled to make most of them reappear as ghosts, because otherwise there would have been no characters left for the last act."

WAGNER NO PRODIGY.

But in spite of all this, Wagner cannot be regarded as a prodigy, the fact being that his individuality was of the kind which matures late—a kind of oak tree in the garden of art. Bach and Beethoven are two conspicuous examples of a like state of things; while Mozart and Mendelssohn may be cited as cases very much the reverse. At ten years of age Mozart was already a feature in European music, and was actually composing operas. At a like age Mendelssohn had begun his career as a composer and had performed in public. In the works of both is found at the very outset, a remarkable maturity. But compare their earlier works with their later ones and you will find no such difference as that which exists in Beethoven's. Nature sent them forth fully equipped. They did a great work and influenced the artistic life of humanity in a wondrous way, but it was by exceptional faculty rather than by force of character and the strife and growth of a profounder life and individuality. This it is which accounts for the all-pervading influence of Bach and Beethoven, and it is difficult to avoid making a comparison, drawn from this line of argument, in favour also of Wagner, whose career was also one of slow growth and unfoldment.

BOYISH PRANKS.

As a boy he displayed a strong love of animals and sympathy with external nature, and this continued to the end of his life. Alongside his own grave in the garden of Wahnfried may be seen to-day a small tombstone which marks the last resting-place of his favourite dog. His high-spirited and generous feeling as a boy is well illustrated by a story which is related of his school-life at Leipzig. A holiday had unexpectedly been granted, to the great delight of the boys, caps were thrown in the air, when Wagner, seizing that of one of his companions, threw it with an unusual effort on to the roof of the school-house, a feat loudly applauded by the rest of the scholars. But there was one dissentient—the unlucky boy whose cap had thus been ruthlessly snatched. He burst into tears. Wagner could never bear to see anyone cry, and with that prompt decision so characteristic of him at all periods of his life, he decided at once to mount the roof for the cap. He re-entered the school-house, rushed upstairs to the cock-loft, climbed out on the roof through a ventilator, and gazed down on the applauding boys. He then set himself to crawl along the steep incline towards the cap. The boys ceased cheering, and drew back in terror. Some hurriedly ran to fetch the schoolmaster. A ladder was brought and carried upstairs to the loft, the boys eagerly crowding behind. Meanwhile Wagner had secured the cap, safely returned to the opening and slid back into the dark loft, just in time to hear excited talking below. He hid himself in a corner behind some boxes, waiting for the placing of the ladder and the schoolmaster who ascended it, when he came from his hiding place, and in an innocent tone inquired what they were looking for—"a bird perhaps?" "Yes; a gallows-bird," was the angry answer of the schoolmaster, who none the less was glad to see the boy safe, for he was a general favourite.

BEETHOVEN'S INFLUENCE.

About this time Wagner chanced to hear at a Gewandhaus concert some music of Beethoven, which created so strong a feeling on what must have been a very impressionable mind, that henceforth this art, too, became inseparably bound up with the boy's life. He began to cultivate in an irregular and impulsive manner the grammar of the art without even the aid of a teacher. Fearing opposition, he kept this to himself, and had composed in a crude way sonatas and other pieces before the family circle became aware of his new departure. Even when a teacher was provided, his natural impulsiveness showed itself in a marked degree, for he would spend his time in writing overtures for grand orchestra, instead of attending to his elementary studies in harmony. It was, however, his good fortune later on to be placed under Theodore Weinlig, one of Bach's successors as cantor of the celebrated Thomas Schule in Leipzig. Weinlig had a genius for teaching, and from him Wagner obtained a solid training, which bore remarkable fruit in after years, for in the scores of many of his works, notably "The Meistersingers," is to be found scholastic and contrapuntal writing second to none which the art of music has yet produced. Towards Beethoven he had more and more come to entertain feelings of almost idolatry. His acquaintance with the works of the Bonn master was most intimate. He had copied with his own hand most of the overtures in score, while of the sonatas, chamber music and songs he had a complete and enthusiastic knowledge.

EARLY COMPOSITIONS.

During this period, that is up to about his twentieth year, he composed a great deal. There is a piano sonata which is printed, a fantasia in F sharp minor, also for piano, a concert overture in D minor, overture to Raupach's "König Enzio," a concert overture with fugue in C major, and a large orchestral symphony in C major. This is the work which has recently been revived, and a few performances given, and it is generally supposed to be the only one of the kind from Wagner's pen. In 1886, however, a sketch of another symphony was discovered among his papers. It is in the key of E major. The first movement is complete. Of the rest only twenty-nine bars of an adagio exist. Wagner himself never mentioned the work, and seems to have forgotten its existence. Competent judges speak of it in the highest terms, and find in its style traces of the influence of Weber as well as of Beethoven.

It may here be mentioned that Wagner's first rough sketches for his works, which usually consist of the vocal parts written out in full, and the orchestral ones roughly indicated on two or more staves, have been preserved, and will (like Beethoven's), doubtless, some day be published. An interesting autobiography, which was withheld until after Wagner's death, has recently been published.

Henceforth Wagner's career expanded into something more than that of the musician. His life-work was to consist in uniting the various elements which constitute what he called the music-drama, and it was in this direction that the individuality of the man gradually unfolded itself.

NO REFORMER OF MUSIC.

There is a prevalent error touching Wagner, namely, that he aimed at being a reformer of music. This is not accurate. It was only in its application to the drama that Wagner's reforms touched music. No doubt, outside the drama, he exerted and still exerts a tremendous musical influence, but this is merely incidental and no part of his design, which was to restore, in the terms of to-day with the splendid accessories of modern life, the condition of things which was enjoyed in ancient Greece; and to this end he laboured unceasingly. Music appears to have been an integral element in the Greek drama, and the peculiar capacity which we find in Wagner is also attributed to Æschylus, who was musical composer as well as poet. Doubtless, what Wagner did musically was very different from that of his great predecessor, yet the principles involved are alike, and in discussing the position and claims of Wagner we must take care to start with an accurate assessment of what his ideas and theories really were.

THE MUSIC OF THE FUTURE.

A half sarcastic, half jocose phrase, "the music of the future" was current a few years ago. Our comic journal "Punch" said such music should be called

"Promissory Notes." Wagner himself never used the phrase. His contention was that the drama, music and the plastic art of painting, architectural design and sculpture should be unified with one common aim, that, namely, of the highest and most complete dramatic expression. This he termed "the art work of the future," and in his later works he strives to exemplify and fulfil this high ideal. One result of Wagner's power to write both drama and music is that his works, so far as the musical colours are concerned, are, to use a homely phrase, "dyed in the wool." Indeed he has left it on record that with him, writing the text of the work was always accompanied by the conception of appropriate musical ideas.

PROGRAMME MUSIC.

There is also another common error which regards Wagner as a writer of what is called programme music, that is music which purports to convey definite physical meanings, a process which Sir Hubert Parry has aptly described as an attempt to make people "see with their ears." This is also a mistake. Wherever in his works Wagner writes purely instrumental movements it is on the abiding principle which Beethoven laid down with regard to his "Pastoral" symphony, that the music is to be regarded as "more the expression of inward feeling than mere picturing." The preludes to the several acts of the music-dramas, "Parsifal," "Tristan," "Lohengrin" and the "Nibelung Ring," abundantly prove this, for it is only in connection with the works themselves as a whole, that these instrumental pieces can be properly estimated. They may be, and in fact are, of profound power and beauty as abstract pieces of music, but only when taken in conjunction with the works of which they form an integral part, is their true significance fully revealed.

THE LEITMOTIV.

Another misconception about Wagner is that he uses musical phrases (leitmotivs) as labels or tickets to identify the characters in his dramas, or, as a critic has humorously put it, "like the lettered ribbons which, issuing from the mouths of figures in mediæval pictures, tell you what they are about." This conception of Wagner's theory is an entire perversion. As has been well said: "They were not invented to announce the entrance of the persons of the play; their duties are not those of footmen and ushers. They stand for deeper things—for the attributes of the play's personages; for the spiritual as well as the material developments of the plot; for the fundamental passions of the story." No doubt Wagner does at times become frankly delineative of natural phenomena, just as did Beethoven.

In both cases, however, the best and truest effects are not then produced, but rather when they write music which nobly suggests, and not merely depicts, certain ideas and events. It is no doubt true that in using the leitmotiv and other unusual musical means Wagner departs from the conventional form of solo, duet and the like, yet he in reality at the same time sets forth a new kind of form, which bears a relation to the drama as a whole, rather than to the smaller, disjunct forms which had hitherto existed in the works of this kind.

THE WAGNER THEATRE AT BAYREUTH.

Without pursuing further the external details of Wagner's career, and with a merely passing mention of compositions like the Holy Supper of the Apostles, a choral work containing music of an astonishing character, and the well-known "Siegfried Idyll," we will now confine ourselves to the consideration of the peculiar features and results of his life-work. Foremost among these is the realisation of his ideal by the completely artistic rendering of his later compositions in a building specially designed and erected for the purpose. I allude, of course, to the now well-known Festspielhaus which was inaugurated in 1876 at Bayreuth, in Bavaria. This place is, in reality, the "outward and visible sign" of that which Wagner strove for, and it is here that many an eager and enthusiastic pilgrim has found artistic rest and satisfaction. The journey is rather a lengthy one. A good route is by Harwich and the Hook of Holland. Thence via Cologne and Frankfort to Nuremberg, whence Bayreuth is reached in a few hours. The Festspielhaus is outside the town on rising ground, quite in the country, and as unlike the ordinary theatre as anything well could be. Wagner is credited with having selected Bayreuth, which is a somewhat out of the way town, for the erection of his ideal house, because of finding there an entire freedom from the blighting influences of fashion. This is true in a sense, yet circumstances had in this case, as in many another, much to do in the matter, for a building was originally designed for erection in the city of Munich, and but for the wrongheadedness of the Munichers, that place would have now enjoyed the distinction, not to say emoluments, which falls to the lot of the small Bavarian town. The Festspielhaus is externally an unpretentious edifice, yet not, as has sometimes been stated, at all ugly. Constructed chiefly of red brick, it is evident that utility has been a main consideration, yet there is nothing inartistic in the design, or at all unpleasant to the eye. An open space in front, from which the carriage and foot roads descend to Bayreuth, affords an ample and pleasant promenade, which may be extended into the woods on either hand. A piazza runs round the outside, from which entry to the house is made by twelve doors, so that the audience to the number of about 1,400, can enter or leave in a few minutes without crush or inconvenience. Every seat in the theatre has an uninterrupted view of the stage, there being no side seats or galleries. From the seats nearest the stage, the auditorium rises tier upon tier, each row being a little longer than the last, so that the whole block presents a wedge-shaped appearance, the narrow end being near the stage. At the commencement of each act the lights are lowered as much as possible, rendering the house itself almost dark. In this way the attention of the audience is concentrated, and the effect immensely heightened. Between the auditorium and the stage is the orchestra. This is a sunken space, the width of the stage, and going partially under it. It is of ample space, holding 110 to 120 performers. Viewed from any part of the auditorium no instrumentalist nor the conductor is visible, and by an ingenious arched screen on both sides of the orchestral space, the very fact that this space exists at all is not apparent to the audience, although it is in reality open and free for the sound to make due effect. On the other hand, those on the stage have an excellent view of the conductor, which, of course, is an absolute necessity in works so complex and difficult as those of Wagner.

WAGNER'S OPERAS AND MUSIC-DRAMAS.

We will now pass in rapid review Wagner's works, and it will be interesting to note how tardy was their recognition, even by musical authorities. "Die Feen" (The Fairies), a very early opera, was never performed during Wagner's lifetime. "Das Liebes-Verbot" (The Novice of Palermo) was only performed once. "Rienzi" was finished in 1840. It was first heard in England in 1879. This work, which is of the spectacular kind, is now frequently performed. "The Flying Dutchman," written in 1841, was first performed two years later, and then laid by for ten years before another performance was given. In London it was not heard until 1870, that is when it was about thirty years old. It is now given hundreds of times annually, and is a most popular work. "Tannhäuser" was written about 1842. It was hardly heard even in Germany for many years, and not in England until 1876. It is now very highly esteemed and often performed, yet at the outset it was misunderstood, and criticisms of an amazing kind were written about it.

CURIOSITIES OF CRITICISM.

A leading English musical authority wrote: "I have never been so blanked, pained and worried, insulted even (the word is not too strong), by a work of pretension as by this same 'Tannhäuser.'" An equally eminent German critic says: "Wagner is no artist, either in taste or creativeness. *I do not believe a single work of his will survive.* 'Tannhäuser' will disappear after the second performance." Yet according to official statistics, "Tannhäuser" was performed two hundred and fifty times during 1890 in Germany alone! The overture, now perhaps the most popular orchestral piece in existence, was pronounced by another critic in 1846 to be "quite atrocious, incredibly awkward in construction, long and tedious." Probably it was the same critic who denounced the overture to "The Flying Dutchman" as an "infernal racket," and declared that it had actually made him seasick. (The story is, of course, one of the sea.) "Lohengrin" was composed in 1847, first performed at Weimar in 1850 and secondly at Wiesbaden in 1853. It was not heard in London until 1875. Wagner himself did not hear it until thirteen years after it was written, owing to his exile for taking part in the Dresden insurrection. To-day "Lohengrin" is one of the most highly esteemed of serious operas, and it is difficult to believe that eminent musical critics such as Hanslick, of Vienna, Henry Chorley, of London, and others, wrote such things as the following about this work: "The composer of 'Lohengrin' is an anti-melodious fanatic, and every new opera of his has become more and more tedious, noisy and abstruse." "The prelude to 'Lohengrin' is but a series of acoustic effects, a cleverly-managed *crescendo*, a persistent tremolo on the first string leading up to a sonorous entry of the brass instruments, and all this without the shadow of an idea. It is an audacious defiance of everything that people have hitherto agreed to call music." "The entire opera from beginning to end does not contain a dozen bars of melody. It is the wildest kind of rambling, utterly destitute of form or sequence. It will attract for a time, but that works after the manner of 'Lohengrin,' which may be described as an opera without music, should take permanent hold on the human soul is to me simply inconceivable." This latter precious utterance, strange as it may seem, is that of none other than the well-known John Hullah, who, in this matter, appears to have gone as far astray as he did in his estimate of the tonic sol-fa movement.

THE "RING."

The "Nibelungen Ring," which consists of four parts, each of large dimensions, is in many respects the most remarkable, as it is the most gigantic, artistic production of our time. It was, so far as Part I ("Rheingold"), Part II ("Die Walküre") and Part III ("Siegfried") are concerned, written from 1850 to 1857, but the completion of the work did not take place till 1874. With it the Festspielhaus at Bayreuth was opened in 1876, and whatever may be the future of the work as a whole, there can be no question that portions of it are of wondrous power and beauty; such scenes, for example, as Wotan's farewell to his goddess-daughter Brünnhilde, and the closing scene of the "Götterdämmerung," wherein the drama is united to music which is no mere accompaniment, but rather a nobly conceived symphonic vesture of tones, gorgeous in colour, and at times touching the utmost bounds of emotional expression. How anyone possessed of a vestige of true musical feeling can fail to recognise the transcendant beauty of such music is past comprehension.

"TRISTAN" AND THE "MEISTERSINGERS."

"Tristan and Isolde" was composed in 1858, but not performed until 1866. Many authorities regard this work as most fully exemplifying Wagner's later method, and a truly remarkable composition it is. The "Meistersingers of Nuremburg," Wagner's one humorous work, was completed in 1867, and performed the following year. Probably Wagner intended it as a satire on the spirit of pedantry, which was such an obstacle, then as now, to artistic progress. The work aims "to chastise manners with a smile."

"PARSIFAL."

"Parsifal," the last, and in many respects the greatest of his creations had been in his mind as early as 1852, and hints appear from time to time in his letters that the subject was occupying his attention. It was not, however, completed till 1882, the first performance taking place the same year at Bayreuth. This is the work which (save as to certain private representations witnessed by Ludwig, King of Bavaria, alone, at Munich) had until recent times never been performed save at Bayreuth. Like the Passion Play at Oberammergau, with which it has something in common, it merits a higher fate than to be made a mere show of. Wagner designates this work a "Bühnenweih Festspiel," and truly it is entitled to the appellation "consecrated," for in it are brought together the ripest results of art, philosophy and religion. The story of "Parsifal" need not be repeated here. It is by this time familiar to all who are interested in the subject, and Wagner's treatment of the legend is generally admitted to present points of the deepest interest, even by those who are not in sympathy with his theories and musical methods.

CONCLUSION.

In conclusion, little or nothing has been said as to Wagner's frailties, but no one who is acquainted with his history will deny their existence. In fact a great deal has already been made of them in certain quarters, and some critics in their anxiety to justify the opposition which they feel to the man and his works have stooped to seek for evidence even in his dressing-room. Wagner's personal eccentricities and specially his fads about wearing apparel are certainly very amusing, but surely his opponents must be hard driven for solid argument when they try to find in such trivialities demonstration of his artistic unworthiness. Time alone can finally determine affairs of this kind, but it may at least be fairly urged that the ever-increasing influence of Wagner's works and ideas among thoughtful people presages for him ultimately a high and enduring place in the Temple of Art.

Richard Wagner was no God (as some unwise partisans almost seem to imply), nor was he (as the savagery of his earlier critics comes very near asserting) a musical devil. Rather, we may take it, viewed as one who, through long years of abuse and neglect, boldly stood up for the principles which he held sacred, and which in the main are now accepted, was he one of the true order of heroes—heroes to whom the world owes a deep debt of gratitude, and whose artistic (though oft unconscious) impulses were in reality the outcome of a creed which is well set forth in the stirring words of the poet:

> Take thou no thought for aught save right and truth,
> Life holds for finer souls no equal prize;
> Honours and wealth are baubles to the wise,
> And pleasure flies on swifter wings than youth:
> If in thy heart thou bearest seeds of hell,
> Though all men smile, yet what shall be thy gain?
> Though all men frown, if truth and right remain,
> Take thou no thought for aught, for all is well.

N. KILBURN.

THE DRAMATIC CONSTRUCTION OF THE "RING."

THE "Ring of the Nibelung" consists of four music-dramas—"Rhinegold," the "Valkyr," "Siegfried" and "The Dusk of the Gods." The "books" of these were written in inverse order. Wagner made a dramatic sketch of the Nibelung myth as early as the autumn of 1848 and between then and the autumn of 1850 he wrote the "Death of Siegfried." This subsequently became "The Dusk of the Gods." Meanwhile Wagner's ideas as to the proper treatment of the myth seem to have undergone a change. "Siegfried's Death" ended simply dramatically, Brünnhilde leading Siegfried to Valhalla. Afterwards Wagner evidently conceived the purpose of connecting the final catastrophe of his trilogy with "The Dusk of the Gods," or end of all things, in northern mythology, and of embodying a profound truth in the action of the music-dramas. This metaphysical significance of the work is believed to be sufficiently explained in the brief synopsis of the plot of the trilogy and in the descriptive musical and dramatic analysis below.

In the autumn of 1850 when Wagner was on the point of sketching out the music of "Siegfried's Death," he recognised that he must lead up to it with another drama, and "Young Siegfried," afterwards "Siegfried" was the result. This in turn he found incomplete, and finally decided to supplement it with the "Valkyr" and "Rhinegold." This backward *modus operandi* he explained to Liszt in a characteristic letter dated Albisbrunn, November 20, 1851.

"Rhinegold" was produced in Munich, at the Hoftheater, September 22, 1869; the "Valkyr" on the same stage, June 26, 1870. "Siegfried" and "The Dusk of the Gods" were not performed until 1876, when they were produced at Bayreuth.

Of the principal characters in the "Ring of the Nibelung," Alberich, the Nibelung, and Wotan, the chief of the gods, are symbolic of greed for wealth and power. This lust leads Alberich to renounce love—the most sacred of emotions—in order that he may rob the Rhine-daughters of the Rhinegold and forge from it the ring which is to make him all-powerful. Wotan by strategy obtains the ring, but, instead of returning it to the Rhine-daughters, he gives it to the giants, Fafner and Fasolt, as ransom for Freia, the goddess of youth and beauty, whom he had promised to the giants as a reward for building Valhalla. Alberich has cursed the ring and all into whose possession it may come. The giants no sooner obtain it than they fall to quarrelling over it, and Fafner slays Fasolt and then retires to a cave in the heart of a forest where, in the form of a dragon, he guards the ring and the rest of the treasure which Wotan wrested from Alberich and also gave to the giants as ransom for Freia. This treasure includes the tarn-helmet, a helmet made of Rhinegold, the wearer of which can assume any guise.

Wotan having witnessed the slaying of Fasolt is filled with dread lest the curse of Alberich be visited upon the gods. To defend Valhalla against the assaults of Alberich and the host of Nibelungs, he begets in union with Erda, the goddess of wisdom, the Valkyrs (chief among them Brünnhilde) who course through the air on superb chargers and bear the bodies of departed heroes to Valhalla, where they revive and aid the gods in warding off the attacks of the Nibelungs. But it is also necessary that the curse-laden ring should be wrested from Fafner and restored through purely unselfish motives to the Rhine-daughters, and the curse thus lifted from the race of the gods. None of the gods can do this because the motives would not be entirely unselfish. Hence, Wotan, for a time, casts off his divinity, and in disguise as Wälse, begets in union with a human woman the Wälsung twins, Siegmund and Sieglinde. Siegmund, he hopes, will be the hero who will slay Fafner and restore the ring to the Rhine-daughters. To nerve him for this task, Wotan surrounds the Wälsungs with numerous hardships. Sieglinde is forced to become the wife of her robber Hunding. Siegmund, storm-driven, seeks shelter in Hunding's hut, where he and his sister, recognising one another, form an incestuous union and escape. Hunding overtakes them and as Siegmund has been guilty of a crime against the marriage vow, Wotan is obliged, at the request of his spouse Fricka, the Juno of northern mythology, to give victory to Hunding. Brünnhilde, contrary to Wotan's command, takes pity on Siegmund, and seeks to shield him against Hunding. For this Wotan causes her to fall into a profound slumber. The hero who will penetrate the barrier of fire with which Wotan has surrounded the rock upon which she slumbers can claim her as his bride.

After Siegmund's death Sieglinde gives birth to Siegfried, a son of their incestuous union, who is reared by one of the Nibelungs, Mime, in the forest where Fafner guards the Nibelung treasure. Mime is seeking to weld the pieces of Siegmund's sword (Nothung or Needful) in order that Siegfried may slay Fafner, Mime hoping to then possess himself of the treasure. But he cannot weld the sword. At last Siegfried, learning that it was his father's weapon, welds the pieces and slays Fafner. His lips having come in contact with his bloody fingers, he is, through the magic power of the dragon's blood, enabled to understand the language of the birds, and a little feathery songster warns him of Mime's treachery. Siegfried slays the Nibelung and is then guided to the fiery barrier around the Valkyr rock. Penetrating this, he comes upon Brünnhilde, and, enraptured with her beauty, he awakens her and claims her as his bride, and she, the virgin pride of the goddess, yielding to the love of the woman, gives herself up to him. He plights his troth with the curse-laden ring which he has wrested from Fafner.

Siegfried goes forth in quest of adventure. On the Rhine lives the Gibichung, Gunther, his sister, Gutrune, and their half-brother, Hagen, the son of the Nibelung, Alberich. Hagen, knowing of Siegfried's coming, plans his destruction in order to regain the ring for the Nibelungs. Therefore, craftily concealing Brünnhilde's and Siegfried's relations from Gunther, he incites a longing in the latter to possess Brünnhilde as his bride. Carrying out a plot evolved by Hagen, Gutrune, on Siegfried's arrival, presents to him a drinking-horn filled with a love-potion. Siegfried drinks, forgets Brünnhilde, and becoming enamoured of Gutrune, asks her in marriage of Gunther. The latter consents provided Siegfried will disguise himself in the Tarnhelmet as Gunther and lead Brünnhilde to him as bride. Siegfried readily agrees, and in the guise of Gunther overcomes Brünnhilde and delivers her to the Gibichung. But Brünnhilde, recognising on Siegfried the ring which her conqueror had drawn from her finger, accuses him of treachery in delivering her, his own bride, to Gunther. The latter, unmasked and also suspicious of Siegfried, conspires with Hagen, and Brünnhilde, who, knowing naught of the love-potion, is roused to a frenzy of hate and jealousy by Siegfried's treachery, to compass the young hero's death. Hagen slays Siegfried during a hunt, and then in a quarrel with Gunther over the ring also kills the Gibichung. Meanwhile Brünnhilde has learned through the Rhine-daughters of the treachery of which she and Siegfried have been the victims. All her jealous hatred of Siegfried yields to her old love for him and a passionate yearning to join him in death. She draws the ring from his finger and throws upon the pyre the torch which ignites it. Then, mounting her steed, she plunges into the flames. One of the Rhine-daughters seizes the curse-laden ring. Hagen rushes into the flooding Rhine, hoping to regain it, but the other

Rhine-daughters grasp him and draw him down into the flood. Not only the flames of the pyre, but a glow which pervades the whole horizon illumines the scene. It is Valhalla being consumed by fire. Through love—the very emotion Alberich renounced in order to gain wealth and power—Brünnhilde has caused the old order of things to pass away and a new and better era to dawn.

The sum of all that has been written concerning the book of "The Ring of the Nibelung" is probably larger than the sum of all that has been written concerning the librettos used by all other composers in their aggregate. What can be said of the ordinary opera libretto beyond Voltaire's remark that "what is too stupid to be spoken is sung"? But "The Ring of the Nibelung" produced vehement discussion. It was attacked and defended, praised and ridiculed, extolled and condemned. And it survived all the discussion it called forth. It was the grandest fact in Wagner's career that he always triumphed. He threw his lance into the midst of his enemies and fought his way up to it. No matter how much opposition his music-dramas excited, they found their way into the repertoire of the leading opera-houses of Germany, and have since their production proved the most popular musico-dramatic works of the time.

It was contended on many sides that a book like

"The Ring of the Nibelung" could not be set to music. Certainly it could not be after the fashion of an ordinary opera. Perhaps people were so accustomed to the books of nonsense which figured as opera librettos that they thought "The Ring of the Nibelung" was so great a work that its action and climaxes were beyond the scope of musical expression. For such, Wagner has placed music on a high level. He has shown that music makes a great drama greater.

One of the most remarkable features of Wagner's works is the author's absorption of the traits of the times in which he wrote. He seems to have gone back to the very time in which the scene of the music-drama is laid and to have himself lived through the events in his plot. Hans Sachs could not have left a more faithful portrayal of life in the Nuremberg of his day than Wagner has given us in "Die Meistersinger." In "The Ring of the Nibelung" he has done more—he has absorbed an imaginary epoch; lived over the days of gods and demi-gods; infused life into mythological figures. "The Rhinegold," which is full of varied interest from its first note to its last, deals entirely with beings by mythology. They are presented true to life—if that expression may be used in connection with beings that never lived—that is to say, they are so vividly drawn that we forget such beings never lived, and take as much interest in their doings and sayings as if they were life-like reproductions of historical characters. Was there ever a love scene more thrilling than that between Siegmund and Sieglinde? It represents the gradations of the love of two souls from its first awakening to its rapturous greeting in full self-consciousness. No one stops to think during that impassioned scene that the close relationship between Siegmund and Sieglinde would in these days have been a bar to their legal union. For all we know, in those moments when the impassioned music of that scene whirls us away in its resistless current, not a drop of related blood courses through their veins. This is a sufficient answer to the sermons that have been preached against the immorality of this scene.

Moreover, as it is by no means dramatically necessary that Siegmund and Sieglinde should be brother and sister, those who hold mythological beings to as strict a moral accountability as they do the people of to-day can imagine that the lovers were strangers or second cousins or anything else—only let them stop preaching sermons. It has been said that we could not be interested in mythological beings—that "The Ring of the Nibelung" lacked human interest. In reply, I say that wonderful as is the first act of "The Valkyr," there is nothing in it to compare in wild and lofty beauty with the last act of that music-drama—especially the scene between Brünnhilde and Wotan.

That there are faults of dramatic construction in "The Ring of the Nibelung" I admit. I have not hesitated to point them out. But there are faults of construction in Shakespeare. What would be the critical verdict if "Hamlet" were now to have its first performance in the exact form in which Shakespeare left it? With all its faults of dramatic construction "The Ring of the Nibelung" is a remarkable drama, full of life and action and logically developed, the events leading up to superb climaxes. Wagner was doubly inspired. He was both a great dramatist and a great musician.

The chief faults of dramatic construction of which Wagner was guilty in "The Ring of the Nibelung" are certain unduly prolonged scenes which are merely episodical—that is, unnecessary to the development of the plot, so that they delay the action and weary the audience to a point which endangers the success of the really sublime portions of the score. Such are the scenes between Wotan and Fricka and Wotan and Brünnhilde in the second act of "The Valkyr"; between Wotan and Mime in the first act of "Siegfried"; between Wotan and Erda in the third act of "Siegfried"; and the Norn scene in the "Dusk of the Gods." In several of these scenes there is a great amount of narrative in the story of events with which we have become familiar being retold in detail, although some incidents which connect the plot of the particular music-drama with that of the preceding one are also related. But, as narrative on the stage makes little impression, and, when it is sung, perhaps none at all, because it cannot be well understood, it would seem as if prefaces to the libretti could have taken the place of these narratives. Certain it is that these long drawn-out scenes did more to retard the popular recognition of Wagner's genius than the activity of hostile critics and musicians. Still, it should be remembered that nowhere, except at Bayreuth, are these music-dramas given as they should be, and that they were composed for performance under the ideal circumstances which prevail there. At Bayreuth the performances begin in the afternoon and there are long waits between the acts, during which you can refresh yourself by a stroll or by the more mundane pleasures of the table. Then, after an hour's relaxation of the mind and of the sense of hearing, you are ready to hear another act. Under these agreeable conditions the faults of dramatic construction are not fatiguing because one remains sufficiently fresh to enjoy the music of the dramatically faulty scenes. Even poor old Wotan's frequent outbursts of grief are not nearly so tedious as they are when the "Ring" is performed elsewhere than at Bayreuth.

Wotan, except in the noble scene with Brünnhilde in the finale of "The Valkyr," is a bore. He is Wagner's one failure—and Wagner's failure was on as colossal a scale as his successes were. Wotan is the chief of the gods, a race marked out by fate for annihilation. Walking in the shadow of impending destruction he would, one might suppose, bear himself with a certain tragic dignity. Instead of this, however, he is constantly bemoaning his fate, and hence strikes one as contemptible rather than as tragic. Moreover, even if his outbursts of grief were tragic instead of ridiculous and wearisome, we could hardly clothe with god-like dignity a character who pursues the female sex—divine, semi-divine and purely human—with the persistency of a mythological Mormon, and has reared a numerous family each member of which would probably find considerable difficulty in identifying his or her mother.

But if Wotan is a failure, Brünnhilde is, on the other hand, Wagner's noblest creation. She takes upon herself the sins of the gods and the Nibelungs, and by her expiation frees the world from the curse of lust for wealth and power. She is a perfect dramatic incarnation of the profound and beautiful metaphysical argument upon which the plot of "The Ring of the Nibelung" is based.

"THE RHINEGOLD."

(DAS RHEINGOLD.)

SCENE I.

At the Bottom of the Rhine.

IN "The Rhinegold" we meet with supernatural beings of German mythology—the Rhine-daughters, Woglinde, Wellgunde and Flosshilde, whose duty it is to guard the precious Rhinegold; Wotan, the chief of the Gods; his spouse, Fricka; Loge, the God of Fire (the diplomat of Valhalla); Freia, the Goddess of Youth and Beauty; her brothers, Donner and Froh; Erda, the all-wise woman; the giants, Fafner and Fasolt; Alberich and Mime, of the race of Nibelungs, cunning, treacherous gnomes who dwell in Nibelheim in the bowels of the earth.

The first scene of "Rhinegold" is laid on the

Rhine, where the Rhine-daughters guard the Rhine-gold.

The work opens with a wonderfully descriptive prelude, which depicts with marvellous art (marvellous because so simple), the transition from the quietude of the water-depths to the wavy life of the Rhine-daughters. The double basses intone E flat. Only this note is heard during four bars. Then three contra bassoons add a B flat. The chord thus formed sounds until the 136th bar. With the sixteenth bar there flows over this seemingly immovable triad, as the current of a river flows over its immovable bed, the MOTIVE OF THE RHINE:

A horn intones this motive. Then one horn after another takes it up until its wave-like tones are heard on the eight horns. On the flowing accompaniment of the violoncellos the motive is carried to the wood-wind. It rises higher and higher, the other strings successively joining in the accompaniment, which now flows on in gentle undulations until the motive is heard on the high notes of the wood-wind, while the violins have joined in the accompaniment.

When the theme thus seems to have stirred the waters from their depth to their surface the curtain rises.

The scene shows the bed and flowing waters of the Rhine, the light of day reaching the depths only as a greenish twilight. The current flows on over rugged rocks and through dark chasms.

Woglinde is circling gracefully around the central ridge of rock. To an accompaniment as wavy as the waters through which she swims, she sings the much-discussed

> Weia! Waga! Woge, du Welle,
> Walle zur Wiege! Wagala weia!
> Wallala, Weiala weia!

Some of these words belong to what may be termed the language of the Rhine-daughters. Looked at in print they seem odd, perhaps even ridiculous. When, however, they are sung to the melody of the Rhine-daughters they have a wavy grace which is simply entrancing. The motive to which they are sung I call the MOTIVE OF THE RHINE-DAUGHTERS:

In wavy sport the Rhine-daughters dart from cliff

to cliff. Meanwhile Alberich has clambered from the depths up to one of the cliffs, and watches, while standing in its shadow, the gambols of the Rhine-daughters. As he speaks to them there is a momentary harshness in the music, whose flowing rhythm is broken. Characteristically descriptive of his discomfiture is the music when, in futile endeavours to clamber up to them, he inveighs against the "slippery slime" which causes him to lose his foothold.

When, after Woglinde, Wellgunde and Flosshilde have in turn gambolled almost within his reach, only to dart away again, he curses his own weakness, you hear the MOTIVE OF THE NIBELUNG'S SERVITUDE:

Swimming high above him, the Rhine-daughters incite him with gleeful cries to chase them. Alberich tries to ascend, but always slips and falls back. Finally, beside himself with rage, he threatens them with clenched fist. The music accompanying this threat is in the typical rhythm of the Nibelung Motive.

Alberich's gaze is attracted and held by a glow which suddenly pervades the waves above him and increases until, from the highest point of the central cliff, a bright golden ray shoots through the water.

Amid the shimmering accompaniment of the violins is heard on the horn the RHINEGOLD MOTIVE:

With shouts of triumph the Rhine-daughters swim around the rock. Their cry, "Rhinegold," is a characteristic motive, heard again later in the cycle, and the new accompanying figure on the violins may also be noted, as later on further reference to it will be necessary. The RHINE-DAUGHTERS SHOUT OF TRIUMPH and the accompaniment to it are as follows:

As the river glitters with golden light the Rhinegold Motive rings out brilliantly on the trumpet. The Nibelung is fascinated by the sheen. The Rhine-daughters gossip with one another, and Alberich thus learns that the light is that of the Rhinegold, and that whoever shapeth a ring from this gold will become invested with great power. Then is heard the RING MOTIVE in the wood-wind:

When Flosshilde bids her sisters cease their prattle, lest some sinister foe should overhear them, the music which accompanied Alberich's threat in the typical Nibelung rhythm reappears for an instant.

Wellgunde and Woglinde ridicule their sister's anxiety, saying that no one would care to filch the gold, because it would give power only to him who abjures or renounces love. The darkly prophetic MOTIVE OF THE RENUNCIATION OF LOVE is heard here. It is sung by Woglinde:

As Alberich reflects on the words of the Rhine-daughters the Ring Motive occurs both in voice and orchestra in mysterious *pianissimo* (like an echo of Alberich's sinister thoughts), and is followed by the Motive of Renunciation. Then is heard the sharp, decisive rhythm of the Nibelung Motive, and Alberich fiercely springs over to the central rock. The Rhine-daughters scream and dart away in different directions. The threatening measures of the Nibelung—this time loud and relentless—and Alberich has reached the summit of the highest cliff.

"Hark, ye floods! Love I renounce for ever!" he cries, and amid the crash of the Rhinegold Motive he seizes the gold and disappears in the depths. With screams of terror the Rhine-daughters dive after the robber through the darkened water, guided by Alberich's shrill, mocking laugh. Waters and rocks sink; as they disappear, the billowy accompaniment sinks lower and lower in the orchestra. Above it rises once more the Motive of Renunciation. The Ring Motive is heard, and then as the waves change into nebulous clouds the billowy accompaniment rises *pianissimo*, until, with a repetition of the Ring Motive, the action passes to the second scene. One crime has already been committed—the theft of the Rhinegold by Alberich. How that crime and the ring which he shapes from the gold inspire other crimes is told in the course of the following scenes of "Rhinegold." Hence the significance of the Ring Motive as a connecting link between the first and second scenes.

Scene II.

An open space on a mountain height near the Rhine.

The dawn illumines a castle with glittering turrets on a rocky height at the back. Through a deep valley between this and the foreground the Rhine flows.

With the opening of the second scene the stately VALHALLA MOTIVE is heard:

This is a motive of superb beauty. It greets us again and again in "Rhinegold" and frequently in the later music-dramas of the cycle. Yet often as it occurs, one hears it with ever-growing admiration. Valhalla is the dwelling of gods and heroes, and its motive is divinely and heroically beautiful. Though it is essentially broad and stately it often assumes a tender mood, like the chivalric gentleness which every true hero feels toward woman. Thus it is at the opening of the second scene, for here this motive, which, when played *forte* or *fortissimo*, is one of the stateliest of musical inspirations, is marked *piano* and *molto dolce*. In *crescendo* and *decrescendo* it rises and falls, as rises and falls with each breath the bosom of the beautiful Fricka who slumbers at Wotan's side.

As Fricka awakens her eyes fall on the castle. In her surprise she calls to her spouse. Wotan dreams on, the Ring Motive, and later the Valhalla Motive being heard in the orchestra, for with the ring Wotan is finally to compensate the Giants for building Valhalla. As he opens his eyes and sees the castle, you hear the Spear Motive, which is a characteristic variation of the Motive of Compact (No. 9). For Wotan should enforce, if needful, the compacts of the Gods with his spear.

Wotan sings of the glory of Valhalla. All through his apostrophe resounds the Valhalla Motive. Fricka reminds him that he has made a compact with the Giants to deliver over to them for their work in building Valhalla, Freia, the Goddess of Youth and Beauty. This introduces on the violoncellos and double basses the MOTIVE OF COMPACT:

A theme more expressive of the binding force of law it is impossible to conceive. It has the inherent dignity and power of the idea of justice.

Then follows a little domestic spar between Wotan and Fricka, Wotan claiming that Fricka was as anxious as he to have Valhalla built, and Fricka answering that she desired to have it erected in order to persuade Wotan to lead a more domestic life. At Fricka's words:

> Halls, bright and gleaming,

the FRICKA MOTIVE is heard for the first time. It is a caressing motive of much grace and beauty:

It is also prominent in Wotan's reply immediately following. When Wotan tells Fricka that he never intended to really give up Freia to the Giants, chromatics, like little tongues of fire, appear in the accompaniment. They are suggestive of the Loge Motive, for, with the aid of Loge, Wotan hopes to trick the Giants. "Then save her at once!" calls Fricka, as Freia enters in hasty flight. At this point is heard the first bar of the Freia Motive combined with the Flight Motive. The MOTIVE OF FLIGHT is as follows:

The following is the FREIA MOTIVE:

I give it here already in full for convenient reference. With Freia's exclamations that the Giants are pursuing her the first suggestion of the Giant Motive appears, and as these "great, hulking fellows" enter, the heavy, clumsy GIANT MOTIVE is heard in its entirety:

Fasolt and Fafner have come to demand that Wotan deliver up to them Freia, according to his promise when they agreed to build Valhalla for him. In the ensuing scene, in which Wotan parleys with the Giants, the Giant Motive, the Valhalla Motive, the Motive of the Compact and the first bar of the Freia Motive figure until Fasolt's threatening words:

> Peace wane when you break your compact,

when there is heard a version of the Motive of Compact characteristic enough to be distinguished as the MOTIVE OF COMPACT WITH THE GIANTS:

The Valhalla, Giant and Freia Motives again are heard until Fafner speaks of the golden apples which grow in Freia's garden. These golden apples are the fruit of which the gods partake in order to enjoy eternal youth. The Motive of Eternal Youth, which now appears, is one of the loveliest in the cycle. It seems as though age could not wither it, nor custom stale its infinite variety. Its first bar is reminiscent of the Ring Motive (No. 6), for there is a subtle relationship between the golden apples of Freia and the Rhinegold. This is the MOTIVE OF ETERNAL YOUTH:

It is finely combined with the Giant Motive at Fafner's words:

Let her forthwith be torn from them all.

Froh and Donner, Freia's brothers, enter hastily to save their sister. As Froh clasps her in his arms, while Donner confronts the Giants, the Motive of Eternal Youth rings out triumphantly on the horns and wood-wind.

But Freia's hope is short-lived. The Motive of the Compact with the Giants, with its weighty import, resounds as Wotan stretches his spear between the hostile groups. For though Wotan desires to keep Freia in Valhalla, he dare not offend the Giants. But at this critical moment he sees his cunning adviser, Loge, approaching. These are Loge's characteristic motives.

LOGE MOTIVE:

MAGIC FIRE MOTIVE:

They are heard throughout the ensuing scene, in which Wotan upbraids Loge for not having discovered something which the Giants would be willing to accept as a substitute for Freia. Loge says he has travelled the world over without finding aught that would compensate man for the renunciation of a lovely woman. At this point is heard the Motive of Renunciation. Then follows Loge's narrative of his wanderings. With great cunning he intends to tell Wotan of the theft of the Rhinegold and of the wondrous worth of a ring shaped from the gold in order to incite the listening Giants to ask for it as a compensation for giving up Freia. Hence Wagner, as Loge, begins his narrative, has blended, with a marvellous sense of musical beauty and dramatic fitness, two phrases: the Freia Motive and the accompaniment to the Rhine-daughters' shout of triumph in the first scene. Whoever will turn to the vocal-piano score, will find the Freia Motive in the treble and the somewhat simplified accompaniment to the cry "Rhinegold" in the bass. This music continues until Loge says that he discovered but one (namely, Alberich) who was willing to renounce love. Then the Rhinegold Motive is sounded tristely in a minor key, and immediately afterward is heard the Motive of Renunciation.

Loge next tells how Alberich stole the gold. All through this portion of the narrative are heard, in the accompaniment, reminiscences of the motives of the first scene. It should be noticed that when Loge gives Wotan the message of the Rhine-daughters, that the chief of the gods wrests the gold from Alberich and restores it to them, the Rhinegold Motive rings out brilliantly in a major key (C major). Loge has already excited the curiosity of the Giants, and when Fafner asks him what power Alberich will gain through the possession of the gold, he dwells upon the magical attributes of the ring shaped from Rhinegold. As Wotan ponders over Loge's words the Ring Motive is heard, for Wotan is planning how he may possess himself of the ring. With true knowledge of human, and especially of feminine nature, Wagner makes Fricka ask if articles of jewellery could be made of gold. As Loge tells her that the possession of the ring will insure Wotan's fidelity to her and that Alberich's Nibelungs are at that moment forging a ring of the Rhinegold, he sings the Fricka Motive (Fricka being the guardian of marriage-fidelity), while, when he refers to the Nibelungs, there is heard for the first time the Nibelung Motive. (The Nibelung Motive will be found [No. 18] at the point when it assumes its due prominence in the score, viz., in the Nibelheim scene). Wotan is evidently strongly bent on wresting the gold from Alberich and retaining it in his own possession instead of restoring it to the Rhine-daughters for, as he stands wrapt in meditation, the Rhinegold Motive is heard in a minor key, and as he asks Loge how he may shape the gold into a ring, we have the Ring Motive. Loge tells Wotan that Alberich has abjured love and already forged the ring. Here the Motive of Renunciation is sounded with a harsh power expressive of Alberich's tyranny, which we are soon to witness.

Loge's diplomacy is beginning to bear results. Fafner tells Fasolt that he deems the possession of the gold more important than Freia. Notice here how the Freia Motive, so prominent when the Giants insisted on her as their compensation, is relegated to the bass, and how the Rhinegold Motive breaks in upon the Motive of Eternal Youth as Fafner and Fasolt again advance toward Wotan, for they now request Wotan to wrest the gold from Alberich and give it to them as ransom for Freia. Wotan refuses, and the Giants, having proclaimed that they will give Wotan until evening to determine upon his course, seize Freia and drag her away. Here the music is highly descriptive. Pallor settles upon the faces of the gods; they seem to have grown older. Alas, they are already affected by the absence of Freia, the Goddess of Youth, whose motives are but palely reflected by the orchestra, as Loge, with cunning alarm, explains the cause of the gods' distress; until Wotan proclaims that he will go with Loge to Nibelheim.

Loge disappears down a crevice in the side of the rock. From it a sulphurous vapour at once issues. When Wotan has followed Loge into the cleft the vapour fills the stage and conceals the remaining characters. The vapours thicken to a black cloud, continually rising upward, until rocky chasms are seen. These have an upward motion, so that the stage appears to be sinking deeper and deeper. During this transformation scene there is an orchestral interlude. First is heard the Loge Motive, four times interrupted by the Motive of Renunciation; the Motive of Servitude is heard during four bars. Then, with a *molto vivace*, the orchestra dashes into the Motive of Flight. Twice the Ring and Rhinegold Motives are heard, the latter appearing the second time with the typical NIBELUNG MOTIVE expressive of the enslaved Nibelungs constantly working at the forge:

The motive accompanies for sixteen bars, during eight of which the rhythm is emphasised by the anvils on the stage, a broad expansion of the Flight Motive. Meanwhile from various distant quarters ruddy gleams of light illumine the chasms, and when the Flight Motive has died away, only the increasing clangour of the smithies is heard from all directions. Gradually the sound of the anvils grows fainter; and, as the Ring Motive resounds like a shout of malicious triumph (expressive of Alberich's malignant joy at his possession of power), there is seen a subterranean cavern apparently of illimitable depth, from which narrow shafts lead in all directions.

Scene III.

The subterranean caverns of Nibelungen.

At the beginning of the third scene we hear again the measures heard when Alberich chased the Rhine-daughters. Alberich enters from a side cleft, dragging after him the shrieking Mime. The latter lets fall the helmet, which Alberich at once seizes. It is the tarnhelmet, made of Rhinegold, the wearing of which enables the owner to become invisible or assume any shape. As Alberich closely examines the tarnhelmet, its motive is heard. This is the Motive of the Tarnhelmet:

To test its power, Alberich puts it on and changes into a column of vapour. He asks Mime if he is visible, and when Mime answers in the negative Alberich cries out shrilly, "Then feel me instead," at the same time making poor Mime writhe under the blows of a visible scourge.

Alberich then departs—still in the form of a vaporous column—to announce to the Nibelungs that they are henceforth his slavish subjects. Mime cowers down with fear and pain. Wotan and Loge enter from one of the upper shafts. Mime tells them how Alberich has become all-powerful through the ring and the tarnhelmet made of the Rhinegold. The motives occurring in Mime's narrative are the Nibelung, Servitude and Ring Motives, the latter in the terse, malignantly powerful form in which it occurred just before the opening of the third scene. Then Alberich, who has taken off the tarnhelmet and hung it from his girdle, is seen in the distance, driving a crowd of Nibelungs before him from the caves below. They are laden with gold and silver, which he forces them to pile up in one place and so form a hoard. He suddenly perceives Wotan and Loge. After abusing Mime for permitting strangers to enter Nibelheim, he commands the Nibelungs to descend again into the caverns in search of new treasure for him. They hesitate. You hear the Ring Motive. Alberich draws the ring from his finger, stretches it threateningly toward the Nibelungs and commands them to obey the ring's master.

The Nibelungs disperse in headlong flight and with Mime rush back into the cavernous recesses. Alberich looks with mistrust upon Wotan and Loge. He asks them what they seek in Nibelheim. Wotan tells him they have heard reports of his extraordinary power and have come to ascertain if they are true. After some parleying, the Nibelung points to the hoard, saying: "It is the merest heap compared to the mountain of treasure to which it shall rise."

Here appears part of the RISING HOARD MOTIVE, which in its complete form is as follows:

Alberich boasts that the whole world will come under his sway (you hear the Ring Motive), that the gods who now laugh and love in the enjoyment of youth and beauty will become subject to him (you hear the Freia Motive); for he has abjured love (you hear the Motive of Renunciation). Hence, even the gods in Valhalla shall dread him (you hear a variation of the Valhalla Motive), and he bids them beware of the time when the night-begotten host of the Nibelungs shall rise from Nibelheim into the realm of daylight (you hear the Rhinegold Motive followed by the Valhalla Motive, for it is through the power gained by the Rhinegold that Alberich hopes to possess himself of Valhalla). Loge cunningly flatters Alberich, and when the latter tells him of the Tarnhelmet feigns disbelief of Alberich's statements. Alberich, to prove their truth, puts on the helmet and transforms himself into a huge serpent. The Serpent Motive expresses the windings and writhings of the monster.

The serpent vanishes and Alberich reappears. When Loge doubts if Alberich can transform himself into something very small, the Nibelung changes into a toad. Now is Loge's chance. He calls to Wotan to set his foot on the toad. As Wotan does so, Loge puts his hand to its head and seizes the Tarnhelm. Alberich is seen writhing under Wotan's foot. Loge binds Alberich; both seize him, drag him to the shaft from which they descended and disappear ascending. The scene now changes in the reverse direction to that in which it changed when Wotan and Loge were descending to Nibelheim. The orchestra accompanies the change of scene. The Ring Motive dies away from crashing *fortissimo* to *piano*, to be succeeded by the dark Motive of Renunciation. Then is heard the clangour of the Nibelung smithies, and amid it the Motive of Flight in its broadly-expanded form. The Giant, Valhalla, Loge and Servitude Motives follow, the last with crushing force as Wotan and Loge emerge from the cleft, dragging the pinioned Alberich with them. His lease of power was brief. He is again in a condition of servitude.

Scene IV.

Open Space on Mountain Heights.

A pale mist still veils the prospect as at the end of the second scene. Loge and Wotan place Alberich on the ground and Loge dances around the pinioned

Nibelung, mockingly snapping his fingers at the prisoner. Wotan joins Loge in his mockery of Alberich. The Nibelung asks what he must give for his freedom. "Your hoard and your glittering gold," is Wotan's answer. Alberich assents to the ransom and Loge frees the gnome's right hand, Alberich raises the ring to his lips and murmurs a secret behest. The Nibelung Motive is heard, combined at first with the Motive of the Rising Hoard, then with the Motive of Servitude and later with both, the Motive of Servitude being played in the right hand, the other two in the left. These three motives continue prominent as long as the Nibelungs emerge from the cleft and heap up the hoard. Then, as Alberich stretches out the ring toward them, they rush in terror toward the cleft, into which they disappear. Alberich now asks for his freedom, but Loge throws the Tarnhelmet on to the heap. Wotan further demands that Alberich also give up the ring. At these words dismay and terror are depicted on Alberich's face. He had hoped to save the ring, but in vain. Wotan tears it from the gnome's finger. Then Alberich, impelled by hate and rage, curses the ring. The MOTIVE OF THE CURSE is as follows:

To it should be added the syncopated measures

expressive of the threatening and ever-active NIBELUNGS' HATE:

Amid the heavy thuds of the Motive of Servitude Alberich vanishes in the cleft.

The mist begins to rise. It grows lighter. The Giant Motive and the Motive of Eternal Youth are heard, for the giants are approaching with Freia. Donner, Froh and Fricka hasten to greet Wotan. Fasolt and Fafner enter with Freia. It has grown clear, except that the mist still hides the distant castle. Freia's presence seems to have restored youth to the gods. While the Motive of the Giant Compact resounds, Fasolt asks for the ransom for Freia. Wotan points to the hoard. With staves the giants measure off a space of the height and breadth of Freia. That space must be filled out with treasure.

Loge and Froh pile up the hoard, but the giants are not satisfied even when the Tarnhelmet has been added.

They wish also the ring to fill out a crevice. Wotan turns in anger away from them. A bluish light glimmers in the rocky cleft to the right, and through it Erda rises to half her height. She warns Wotan against retaining possession of the ring. The motives prominent during the action preceding the appearance of Erda will be readily recognised. They are the Giant Compact Motive combined with the Nibelung Motive (the latter combined with the Giant Motive and Motive of the Hoard) and the Ring Motive, which breaks in upon the action with tragic force as Wotan refuses to give up the ring to the giants. The ERDA MOTIVE bears a strong resemblance to the Rhine Motive:

The syncopated notes of the Nibelung's malevolence, so threateningly indicative of the harm which Alberich is plotting, are also heard in Erda's warning. Wotan, heeding her words, throws the ring upon the hoard. The giants release Freia, who rushes joyfully towards the gods. Here the Freia Motive, combined with the Flight Motive, now no longer agitated but joyful, rings out gleefully. Soon these motives are interrupted by the Giant and Nibelung Motives, there being added to these later the motive of the Nibelung's Hate and the Ring Motive. Alberich's curse is already beginning its dread work. The giants dispute over the spoils, their dispute waxes to strife, and at last Fafner slays Fasolt and snatches the ring from the dying giant. As the gods gaze horror-stricken upon the scene, the Curse Motive resounds with crushing force. Loge congratulates Wotan that he should have given up the curse-laden ring. His words are accompanied by the Motive of the Nibelungs' Hate. Yet even Fricka's caresses, as she asks Wotan to lead her into Valhalla, cannot divert the god's mind from dark thoughts, and the Curse Motive accompanies his gloomy, curse-haunted reflections.

Donner ascends to the top of a lofty rock. He gathers the mists about him until he is enveloped by a black cloud. He swings his hammer. There is a flash of lightning, a crash of thunder, and lo! the cloud vanishes. A rainbow bridge spans the valley to Valhalla, which is illumined by the setting sun. The DONNER MOTIVE is as follows:

Wotan eloquently greets Valhalla, and then, taking Fricka by the hand, leads the procession of the gods into the castle.

The music of this scene is of wondrous eloquence and beauty. Six harps are added to the ordinary orchestral instruments, and as the variegated bridge is seen their arpeggios shimmer like the colours of the rainbow around the broad, majestic RAINBOW MOTIVE:

Then the stately Valhalla Motive resounds as the gods gaze, lost in admiration, at the Valhalla. It gives way to the Ring Motive as Wotan speaks of the day's ills; and then as he is inspired by the idea of begetting a race of demi-gods to conquer the Nibelungs, there is heard for the first time the SWORD MOTIVE.

But the cunning Loge knows that the curse must do its work, even if not until the distant future; and hence as he remains in the foreground looking after the gods, the Loge and Ring Motives are heard.

The cries of the Rhine-daughters greet Wotan. They beg him to restore the ring to them. But Wotan is deaf to their entreaties. He preferred to give the ring to the giants rather than forfeit Freia.

The Valhalla Motive swells to a majestic climax and the gods enter the castle. Amid shimmering arpeggios the Rainbow Motive resounds. The gods have attained the height of their glory—but the Nibelung's curse is still potent, and it will bring woe upon all who have possessed or will possess the ring until it is restored to the Rhine-daughters. Fasolt was only the first victim of Alberich's curse.

"THE VALKYR."

(DIE WALKÜRE.)

WOTAN'S enjoyment of Valhalla was destined to be short-lived. Filled with dismay by the death of Fasolt in the combat of the Giants for the accursed Ring, and impelled by a dread presentiment that the force of the curse would be visited upon the gods, he descended from Valhalla to the abode of the all-wise woman, Erda. We must assume that matrimonial obligations were not strictly enforced among the gods. It may have been inferred from Fricka's anxiety to have Valhalla built in order to induce Wotan to lead a more domestic life, that the chief god was an old offender against the marriage vow, for though Fricka was the guardian goddess of connubial virtue, she does not seem to have able to hold her spouse in check. To say the least, the chief god was very promiscuous in his attentions to the gentler sex. Thus his visit to Erda was not entirely unremunerative, for while he could not obtain from her a forecast of the future of the gods, she bore him nine daughters. These were the Valkyrs, headed by Brünnhilde—the wild horsewomen of the air, who on winged steeds bore the dead heroes to Valhalla, the warrior's heaven. With the aid of the Valkyrs and the heroes they gathered to Valhalla, Wotan hoped to repel any assault upon his castle by the enemies of the gods.

But though the host of heroes grew to a goodly number the terror of Alberich's curse still haunted the chief of the gods. He might have freed himself from it had he returned the ring and helmet made of Rhinegold, to the Rhine-daughters from whom Alberich filched it; but in his desire to persuade the giants to relinquish Freia, whom he had promised to them as a reward for building Valhalla, he, having wrested the Ring from Alberich, gave it to the Giants instead of returning it to the Rhine-daughters. He saw the Giants contending for the possession of the Ring and saw Fasolt slain—the first victim of Alberich's curse. He knows that the giant Fafner, having assumed the shape of a huge serpent, now guards the Nibelung treasure, which includes the Ring and the Tarnhelmet, in a cave in the heart of a dense forest. How shall the Rhinegold be restored to the Rhine-daughters?

Wotan hopes that this may be consummated by a human hero, who free from the lust for power which obtains among the gods, shall with a sword of Wotan's own forging, slay Fafner, gain possession of the Rhinegold and restore it to its rightful owners, thus righting Wotan's guilty act and freeing the gods from the curse. To accomplish this, Wotan, in human guise as Wälse begets in wedlock with a woman the twins Siegmund and Sieglinde. How the curse of Alberich is visited upon these is related in "The Valkyr."

The dramatis personæ in "The Valkyr" are Brünnhilde and her eight sister Valkyrs, Fricka, Sieglinde, Siegmund, Hunding (the husband of Sieglinde) and Wotan. The action begins after the marriage of Sieglinde to Hunding. The earlier events in the lives of the two Wälsungs we learn of in the narratives of Siegmund and Wotan respectively in the first and second acts of "The Valkyr." Of course, the Wälsungs are in ignorance of the divinity of their father. They know him only as Wälse.

ACT I.

Interior of Hunding's dwelling.

Prelude and Scene I.

The introduction to "The Valkyr" is very different in character from that to "The Rhinegold." In that the Rhine flowing peacefully toward the sea and the innocent gambols of the Rhine-daughters were musically depicted. But "The Valkyr" opens in storm and stress. It is as though the peace and happiness of the first scene of the cycle had vanished from the earth with Alberich's abjuration of love, his theft of the gold and Wotan's equally treacherous crime. This vorspiel is a masterly representation in tone of a storm gathering for its last infuriated onslaught. There is majestic force in its climax. The elements are unloosed. The wind swoops through the forest. Lightning flashes in jagged streaks across the black heavens. There is a crash of thunder and the storm has spent its force.

Two leading motives are employed in this introduction. They are the STORM MOTIVE and the DONNER MOTIVE (No. 24). The STORM MOTIVE is as follows:

These themes are as elementary as that of the Fifth Symphony. From the theme of that symphony Beethoven developed a work which by many is considered his grandest. Similarly Wagner has composed, with the use of only the two motives named, the most stupendous storm music we have—not even excepting the storm of the "Pastorale." I call the attention of those who still labour under the error that Wagner's methods are obscure and involved to the vorspiel to "The Valkyr."

In the early portion of this vorspiel only the string instruments are used. Gradually the instrumentation grows more powerful. With the climax we have a tremendous *ff* on the contra tuba and two tympani, followed by the crash of the Donner Motive on the wind instruments.

The storm then gradually dies away. Before it has quite passed over, the curtain rises, revealing the large hall of Hunding's dwelling. This hall is built around a huge ash-tree, whose trunk and branches pierce the roof, over which the foliage is supposed to spread. There are walls of rough-hewn boards, here and there hung with large plaited and woven hangings. In the right foreground is a large open hearth; back of it in a recess is the larder, separated from the hall by a woven hanging, half drawn. In the background is a large door. A few steps in the left foreground lead up to the door of an inner room. The furniture of the hall is primitive and rude. It consists chiefly of a table, bench and stools in front of the ash-tree. Only the light of the fire on the hearth illumines the room; though occasionally its fitful gleam is slightly intensified by a distant flash of lightning from the departing storm.

The door in the background is opened from without. Siegmund, supporting himself with his hand on the bolt, stands in the entrance. He seems exhausted. His appearance is that of a fugitive who has reached the limit of his powers of endurance. Seeing no one in the hall, he staggers toward the hearth and sinks upon a bearskin rug before it, with the exclamation:

> "Whose hearth this may be,
> Here I must rest me."

In an Italian opera we should probably have had at this point a very amusing illustration of the total disregard for dramatic fitness which characterises the old-fashioned opera. Siegmund, though supposed to be exhausted by his flight through the storm, would have had strength enough left to stand near the footlights and sing an aria with the regulation bravura passages, and if he got enough applause, to sing it over again. Then only would he sink down upon the rug exhausted, but whether from singing or from his flight through the storm we should be unable to say. Wagner's treatment of this scene is masterly. As Siegmund stands in the entrance we hear the SIEGMUND MOTIVE:

This is a sad, weary strain on the violoncellos and

basses. It seems the wearier for the burden of an accompanying figure on the horns, beneath which it seems to stagger as Siegmund staggers toward the hearth. Thus the music not only reflects Siegmund's weary mien, but accompanies most graphically his weary gait. Perhaps Wagner's intention was more metaphysical. Maybe the burden beneath which the Siegmund Motive staggers is the curse of Alberich. It is certainly (as we shall see) through that curse that Siegmund's life has been one of storm and stress.

When the storm-beaten Wälsung has sunk upon the rug the Siegmund Motive is followed by the Storm Motive, *pp*—and the storm has died away. The door of the room to the left opens and Sieglinde appears. She has heard someone enter, and thinking her husband has returned has come into the hall to meet him. Seeing a stranger stretched upon the bearskin rug she approaches and bends compassionately over him.

Her compassionate action is accompanied by a new motive, which by Wagner's commentators has been entitled the Motive of Compassion. But it seems to me to have a further meaning as expressing the sympathy between two souls, a tie so subtle that it is at first invisible even to those whom it unites. Siegmund and Sieglinde, it will be remembered, belong to the same race; and though they are at this point of the action unknown to one another, yet, as Sieglinde bends over the hunted, storm-beaten Siegmund, that subtle sympathy causes her to regard him with more solicitude than would be awakened by any other unfortunate stranger. Hence I have called this motive the MOTIVE OF SYMPATHY —taking sympathy in its double meaning of compassion and affinity of feeling:

The beauty of this brief phrase is enhanced by its unpretentiousness. It wells up from the orchestra as spontaneously as pity mingled with sympathetic sorrow wells up from the heart of a gentle woman. As it is Siegmund who has awakened these feelings in Sieglinde, the Motive of Sympathy is heard simultaneously with the Siegmund Motive.

Siegmund, suddenly raising his head, ejaculates: "Water, water!" Sieglinde hastily snatches up a drinking-horn, and, having quickly filled it at a spring near the house, swiftly returns and hands it to Siegmund. As though new hope were engendered in Siegmund's breast by Sieglinde's gentle ministration the Siegmund Motive rises higher and higher, gathering passion in its upward sweep and then, combined again with the Motive of Sympathy, sinks to an expression of heartfelt gratitude. This passage is scored entirely for strings. Yet no composer, except Wagner, has evoked from a full orchestra sounds richer or more sensuously beautiful.

Siegmund drinks, and then hands the drinking-horn back to Sieglinde. As his look falls upon her features he regards them with growing interest. That strange presentiment of affinity is awakened in his breast. But in him, the storm-beaten fugitive, the emotion called forth by Sieglinde's gentle acts is deeper than sympathy of feeling. We hear versions of the Siegmund Motive and the Motive of Flight (No. 11). But the former is no longer weary and despairing, nor the latter precipitate. It seems as though Siegmund, having found a haven of rest, were recalling his life's vicissitudes with that feeling of sadness:

> Which is not akin to pain,
> And resembles sorrow only
> As the mist resembles rain.

These reminiscences are followed by the LOVE MOTIVE, one of the most tenderly expressive phrases ever penned:

The melody in the entire passage (that is, in the version of the Siegmund and Flight Motives and in the Love Motive) is played by a single violoncello, and thus is invested with a mournful beauty which seems the musical expression of the thought in the lines from Longfellow I have just quoted.

The version of the Motive of Flight preceding the Love Motive is as follows:

The Love Motive is the mainspring of this act. For this act tells the story of love from its inception to its consummation. Similarly in the course of this act the Love Motive rises by degrees of intensity from an expression of the first tender presentiment of affection to the very ecstasy of love.

Siegmund asks with whom he has found shelter, Sieglinde replies that the house is Hunding's, and she his wife, and requests Siegmund to await her husband's return:

> "Weaponless am I:
> The wounded guest,
> He will surely give shelter,"

is Siegmund's reply. With anxious celerity Sieglinde asks him to show her his wounds. But refreshed by the draught of cool spring water and with hope revived by her sympathetic presence, he gathers force, and raising himself to a sitting posture, exclaims that his wounds are but slight; his frame is still firm, and had sword and shield been half so firm he would not have fled from his foes. His strength was spent in flight through the storm; but the night that sank on his vision has yielded again to the sunshine of Sieglinde's presence.

At these words the Motive of Sympathy rises like a sweet hope. Sieglinde fills the drinking-horn with mead and offers it to Siegmund. He asks her to take the first sip. She does so and then hands it to him. His eyes rest upon her while he drinks. As he returns the drinking-horn to her there are traces of deep emotion in his mien. He sighs and gloomily bows his head. The action at this point is most expressively accompanied by the orchestra. Specially noteworthy are an impassioned upward sweep of the Motive of Sympathy as Siegmund regards Sieglinde with traces of deep emotion in his mien; the Motive of Flight as he sighs, thinking perhaps that misfortune will soon part them; and the sad, weary Siegmund Motive as he bows his head.

In a voice trembling with emotion Siegmund tells her that she has harboured one whom misfortune follows whithersoever he wends his footsteps. Lest misfortune should through him enter her dwelling he will depart. With firm determined strides he has reached the door, when Sieglinde, forgetting all in her growing passion, calls after him:

> "Then tarry here!
> Not bringest thou woe thither
> Where sorrow already reigns."

Upon Sieglinde as one of the Wälsung race, rests the curse of Alberich. Her words are followed by a phrase freighted with woe, the Motive of the Wälsung Race or the WÄLSUNG MOTIVE:

Like the Siegmund Motive it is intoned by the violoncellos and basses.

Siegmund turns and gazes searchingly into her features. Sadly, and as though shamed by her outburst of feeling, she lets her eyes sink toward the ground. Siegmund returns. He leans against the hearth. His calm, steady gaze rests upon her. She slowly raises her eyes to his. In long silence and with deep emotion they regard each other. In the musical accompaniment to this scene several motives are very effectively combined. Its basis is appropriately formed by the Wälsung Motive. Over this rises the Motive of Sympathy. We then hear the Wälsung and Flight Motives combined; next the Love Motive, and finally the Siegmund Motive.

SCENE II.

Sieglinde is the first to start from the reverie. She hears Hunding leading his horse to the stall. The music suddenly changes in character. Like a premonition of Hunding's entrance we hear the HUND-

ING MOTIVE, *pp.* Then as Hunding, armed with spear and shield, stands upon the threshold, this HUNDING MOTIVE—as dark, forbidding and portentous of woe to the two Wälsungs as Hunding's sombre visage—resounds with dread power on the tubas :

Calmly and firmly Siegmund meets Hunding's scrutiny. Sieglinde tells her husband that she found Siegmund exhausted near the hearth and refreshed him with mead. Hunding bids her prepare the meal. He does this with a semblance of graciousness. While preparing the meal Sieglinde's glance again and again wanders over to Siegmund. Hunding, scanning the stranger's features, detects in them a resemblance to those of Sieglinde. "How like unto her!" he mutters to himself, his words being followed by the Motive of Compact (No. 9)—for Wotan's surrender of the Rhinegold to the giants in order to thus fulfil his compact with them for building Walhalla necessitated the creation of the Wälsung race, through a scion of which Wotan hopes to see the Rhinegold restored to the Rhine-daughters.

The table is spread. The three seat themselves. Hunding questions Siegmund as to his name. Siegmund gazes thoughtfully before him. Sieglinde regards him with noticeable interest. Hunding, who has observed both, bids Siegmund gratify Sieglinde's curiosity, and she, little suspecting her husband's thoughts, urges Siegmund to tell his story. Siegmund in the narrative which follows conceals his identity and that of his father, evidently through fear that Hunding may be one of the numerous enemies of the Wälsungs. He calls himself Woeful and his father Wolf. He tells how one day in his boyhood, after hunting with his father, they returned to find their dwelling in ashes, his mother's corpse among the ruins and no trace of his twin sister. Hunted by enemies, he and his father lived a wild life in the forest until in one of the combats they were separated. In vain he sought for a trace of his father. He found only a wild wolf's fur.*

Siegmund sought to mingle with men and women, but wherever he went misfortune and strife followed him. His last combat was in behalf of a maiden whose brothers were forcing her to wed a man she loved not. He defended her till shield and sword

---

* At this point you hear the Walhalla Motive (No. 8), for the father was none other than Wotan, known to his human descendants only as Wälse. In Wotan's narrative in the next act it will be found that Wotan purposely created these misfortunes for Siegmund in order to strengthen him for his task.

were in splinters. Then he fled, reaching Hunding's house when almost dead from exhaustion.

The story of Siegmund is told in melodious recitative. It is not a melody in the old-fashioned meaning of the term, but it fairly teems with melodiousness. It will have been observed that incidents very different in kind are related by Siegmund. It would be impossible to treat this narrative with sufficient variety of expression in a melody. But in Wagner's melodious recitative the musical phrases reflect every incident narrated by Siegmund. For instance, when Siegmund tells how he went hunting with his father, there is joyous freshness and abandon in the music which, however, suddenly sinks to sadness as he narrates how they returned and found the Wälsung dwelling devastated by enemies. We hear also the Hunding Motive at this point, which thus indicates that those who brought this misforune upon the Wälsungs were none other than Hunding and his kinsmen. As Siegmund tells how, when he was separated from his father, he sought to mingle with men and women, you hear the Love Motive, while his description of his latest combat is accompanied by the rhythm of the Hunding Motive. Those whom Siegmund slew were Hunding's kinsmen. Thus Siegmund's dark fate has driven him to seek shelter in the house of the very man who is the arch-enemy of his race and is bound by the laws of kinship to avenge on Siegmund the death of kinsmen. These are some of the salient points of Siegmund's narrative concerning which more might be written. To me this portion of the score, whether we consider it in connection with the words, or as pure music, has far more value than other more popular passages, for instance, Siegmund's love song; though for some years to come probably the mass of the public will continue to regard the latter as the "gem of the opera."

As Siegmund concludes his narrative the Wälsung Motive is heard. Gazing with ardent longing toward Sieglinde, he says:

> "Now know'st thou, questioning wife,
> Why 'Peaceful' is not my name."

These words are sung to a lovely phrase. Then, as Siegmund rises and strides over to the hearth while Sieglinde, pale and deeply affected by his tale, bows her head, there is heard on the horns, bassoons, violas and violoncellos a motive expressive of the heroic fortitude of the Wälsungs in struggling against their fate. It is the MOTIVE OF THE WÄLSUNGS'S HEROISM:

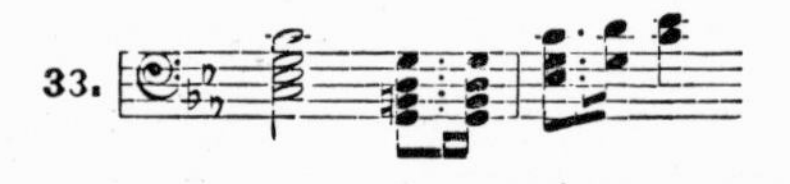

It is followed by an effective variation of the

Wälsung Motive, the whole concluding beautifully with the phrase last sung by Siegmund.

Hunding's sombre visage darkens more deeply as he rises. His were the kinsmen of the woman for whom Siegmund fought. The laws of hospitality make it imperative that he should give the Wälsung shelter for that night, but he bids Siegmund be ready for combat in the morn. He commands Sieglinde to prepare his night-draught. She is seen to throw spices into the horn. As she is about to enter the inner chamber she turns her eyes longingly upon the weaponless Siegmund and, having attracted his attention, fixes her gaze significantly upon a spot on the trunk of the ash-tree. As her look falls upon the tree the Sword Motive (No. 26) is heard.

Scene III.

When Hunding has followed Sieglinde, Siegmund sinks down upon the bearskin near the hearth and broods over his fate. His gloomy thoughts are accompanied by the threatening rhythm of the Hunding Motive and the Sword Motive *in a minor key*, for Siegmund is still weaponless. When giving vent to his thoughts, he exclaims:

"A sword my father did promise!"

the Motive of Compact is heard. But the promise appears to have been delusive and so the Compact

Motive soon loses itself in the threatening rhythm of the Hunding Motive. With the strength of desperation Siegmund invokes Wälse's aid. He cries:

"Wälse! Wälse! Where is thy sword?"

The Sword Motive rings out like a shout of triumph. The embers of the fire collapse. In the glare that for a moment falls upon the ash tree the hilt of a sword whose blade is buried in the trunk of the tree is discernible at the point upon which Sieglinde's look last rested. While the Motive of the Sword gently rises and falls, like the coming and going of a lovely memory, Siegmund apostrophises the sheen as the reflection of Sieglinde's glance. The embers die out. Night falls upon the scene. But in Siegmund's thoughts the memory of that pitying, loving look glimmers on.

The Motive of Sympathy hastening like quick footsteps—and Sieglinde is by Siegmund's side. She has given Hunding a sleeping potion. She will point out a weapon to Siegmund—a sword. If he can wield it she will call him the greatest hero, for only the mightiest can wield it. The music quickens with the subdued excitement in the breasts of the two Wälsungs. You hear the Sword Motive, and above it, on horns, clarinet and oboe, a new motive—that of the WÄLSUNGS'S CALL TO VICTORY:

for Sieglinde hopes that with the sword the stranger, who has awakened so quickly love in her breast, will overcome Hunding. This motive has a resistless, onward sweep. Sieglinde, amid the strains of the stately Walhalla Motive, followed by the Sword Motive, narrates the story of the sword. While Hunding and his kinsmen were feasting in honour of her forced marriage with him, an aged stranger entered the hall. The men knew him not and shrank from his fiery glance. But upon her his look rested with tender compassion. With a mighty thrust he buried a sword up to its hilt in the trunk of the ash tree. Whoever drew it from its sheath, to him it should belong. The stranger went his way. One after another the strong men tugged at the hilt—but in vain. Then she knew who the aged stranger was and for whom the sword was destined.

The Sword Motive rings out like a joyous shout, and Sieglinde's voice mingles with the triumphant notes of the Wälsung's Call to Victory as she turns to Siegmund:

> "Oh, I found in thee
> The friend in need!"

The Motive of the Wälsungs's Heroism, now no

longer full of tragic import, but forceful and defiant—and Siegmund holds Sieglinde in his embrace. There is a rush of wind. The woven hangings flap and fall. As the lovers turn, a glorious sight greets their eyes. The landscape is illumined by the moon. Its silver sheen flows down the hills and quivers along the meadows whose grasses tremble in the breeze. All nature seems to be throbbing in unison with the hearts of the lovers. The voices of spring—the season when love opens like the buds—are whispered to Siegmund by the orchestra, and as he hears them he greets Sieglinde with the LOVE SONG:

The Love Motive, impassioned, irresistible, sweeps through the harmonies—and Love and Spring are united. The Love Motive also pulsates through Sieglinde's ecstatic reply after she has given herself fully up to Siegmund in the Flight Motive—for before his coming her woes have fled as winter flies before the coming of the spring. With Siegmund's exclamation:

> "Oh, wondrous vision!
> Rapturous woman!"

there rises from the orchestra like a vision of loveliness the Motive of Freia (No. 12), the Venus of

German mythology. In its embrace it folds this pulsating theme:

which throbs on like a long love-kiss until it seemingly yields to the blandishments of this caressing phrase:

This throbbing, pulsating, caressing music is succeeded by a moment of repose. While the Walhalla Motive is heard Sieglinde gazes searchingly into Siegmund's features. They are strangely familiar to her. The Love Motive weaves itself around Siegmund's words as he also discovers familiar traces in Sieglinde's mien. Sieglinde once saw her face reflected in the brook—it seems reflected in Siegmund's features. She has heard his voice—it was when she heard the echo of her own voice in the forest. His look has already gleamed upon her—it was when the stranger gazed upon her before he thrust the sword into the trunk of the ash tree.* Was Wolf really his father—is Woeful really his name?

* Notice here the combination of Sword and Wälsung's Heroism motives, followed by a combination of Sword and Walhalla motives.

Siegmund proclaims that his father was a wolf to timid foxes. But he whose glance gleamed as gleams Sieglinde's glance was Wälse. Then, while the orchestra fairly seethes with excitement, Sieglinde, almost beside herself, calls jubilantly to him who came to her a stranger out of the storm:

> "Was Wälse thy father,
> And art thou a Wälsung!
> Thrust he for thee
> His sword in the tree!
> Then let me name thee
> As I love thee—
> Siegmund, I call thee!"

Siegmund leaps upon the table. The Motive of the Wälsung's Heroism rings out in defiance of the enemies of the race. The Sword Motive—and he has grasped the hilt; the Motive of Compact, ominous of the fatality which hangs over the Wälsungs; the Motive of Renunciation, with its threatening import; then the Sword Motive—brilliant like the glitter of refulgent steel—and Siegmund has unsheathed the sword. The Wälsungs's Call to Victory, like a song of triumph; a superb upward sweep of the Sword Motive; the Love Motive, now rushing onward in the very ecstasy of passion, and Siegmund holds in his embrace Sieglinde—sister and bride!

Act II.

A Wild Rocky Place.

Prelude and Scene I.

"The Vorspiel": with an upward rush of the Sword Motive, resolved into 9-8 time, the orchestra dashes into the Flight Motive. The Sword Motive in this 9-8 rhythm closely resembles the Motive of the Valkyrs' Ride (No. 37), and the Flight Motive in the version in which it appears is much like the Valkyrs' Shout (No. 36). The Ride and the Shout are heard in the course of the vorspiel, the former with tremendous force on trumpets and trombones as the curtain rises upon a wild, rocky mountain pass, at the back of which, through a natural rock-formed arch, a gorge slopes downward. In the foreground stands Wotan, armed with spear, shield and helmet. Before him is Brünnhilde in the superb costume of the Valkyrs. The stormy spirit of the Vorspiel pervades the music of Wotan's command to Brünnhilde that she bridle her steed for battle and spur it to the fray to do combat for Siegmund against Hunding. Brünnhilde greets Wotan's command with the weirdly joyous SHOUT OF THE VALKYRS:

It is the cry of the wild horsewomen of the air, coursing through storm-clouds, their shields flashing back the lightning, their voices mingling with the shrieks of the tempest. Weirder, wilder joy has never found expression in music. The tone-colours employed by Wagner are so graphic that one sees the streaming manes of the steeds of the air and the streaks of lightning playing around their riders, and hears the whistling of the winds. It is a marvellous tone-picture, equalled only by other creations of its creator.

The accompanying figure is based on the Motive of the RIDE OF THE VALKYRS:

Brünnhilde, having leapt from rock to rock, to the highest peak of the mountain, again faces Wotan, and with delightful banter calls to him that Fricka is approaching in her ram-drawn chariot. At the words:

"Ha! how she wields her golden scourge,"

we hear a version of the Motive of Servitude (No. 3), which occurs again when Fricka has appeared and descended from her chariot and advances towards Wotan, Brünnhilde having meanwhile disappeared behind the mountain height. Wotan, through his guilt, has become the slave of his evil conscience, and the Motive of Servitude now stands for the remorseless energy with which crime pursues its perpetrator.

The ensuing scene between Wotan and Fricka has been subjected to an immense amount of criticism and ridicule. Even Wagnerian commentators are somewhat timid in their references to it. Von Wolzogen dismisses it with a few words. It is therefore with some pride that I point to an American criticism which is justly appreciative. I refer to the letters which Mr. J. R. G. Hassard contributed from Bayreuth to the "Tribune" in 1876. The lucidity of Mr. Hassard's treatment of the subject, the felicity of his diction, his thorough comprehension of Wagner's theory and his appreciation of its artistic beauty make these letters worthy to be ranked among the most important contributions to the musical literature of the day. This scene between Wotan and Fricka Mr. Hassard calls "another of those great dramatic scenes, full of fine discriminations, of forcible declamation, and of almost illimitable suggestiveness, which alone would point out Wagner as the greatest of writers for the musical stage."

The plain facts concerning this scene are these: it is somewhat long, and hence, from a dramatic point of view, perhaps too extended, as it delays the action. But if it may be *partially* condemned dramatically, it must be *entirely* and unreservedly praised musically. Indeed it is musically so fine that to an intelligent listener all sense of lengthiness disappears. Fricka is the protector of the marriage vow, and as such she has come in anger to demand from Wotan vengeance in behalf of Hunding. As she advances hastily toward Wotan, her angry, passionate demeanour is reflected by the orchestra, and this effective musical expression of Fricka's ire is often heard in the course of the scene. When near Wotan she moderates her pace and her angry demeanour gives way to sullen dignity. This change is also graphically depicted in the orchestra in a phrase based on the fourth bar of the Fricka motive.

Wotan feigns ignorance of the cause of Fricka's agitation and asks what it is that harasses her. Her reply is preceded by the stern Hunding motive. She tells Wotan that she, as the protectress of the sanctity of the marriage vow, has heard Hunding's voice calling for vengeance upon the Wälsung twins. Her words, "His voice for vengeance is raised," are set to a phrase strongly suggestive of Alberich's curse. It seems as though the avenging Nibelung were pursuing Wotan's children and thus striking a blow at Wotan himself through Fricka. The Love motive breathes through Wotan's protest that Siegmund and Sieglinde only yielded to the magic of the spring night. There is a superbly forceful strain when Wotan exclaims:

> "For when strong spirits are rampant
> I rouse them ever to strife."

The wrathful phrase expressive of Fricka's anger, heard at the beginning of the scene, introduces her invective against the nuptial union of brother and sister which reaches a stormy climax with her exclamation:

> "When was it heard of,
> That brother and sister
> Were lovers?"

With the cool impudence of a nineteenth-century husband, who is bandying words into a domestic spat, Wotan replies:

> "Now it's been heard of!"

Wotan argues that Siegmund and Sieglinde are true lovers, and Fricka should smile instead of venting her wrath on them. The motive of the Love Song, the Love Motive and the caressing phrase heard in the love scene are beautifully blended with Wotan's words. In strong contrast to these motives is the music in Fricka's outburst of wrath, introduced by the phrase reflecting her ire, which is repeated several times in the course of this episode. This is followed at the words:

> "Why mourn I thus o'er virtue and vows,"

by a phrase which has a touch of pathos, for she is complaining of Wotan's faithlessness. When she upbraids him for his lapses with Erda, the results of which were the Valkyrs, you hear the motive of the Ride of the Valkyrs. The passage concludes with a paroxysm of rage, Fricka bidding Wotan complete his work and let the Wälsungs in their triumph trample her under their feet. Wotan explains to her why he begat the Wälsung race and the hopes he has founded upon it. But Fricka mistrusts him. What can mortals accomplish that the gods, who are far mightier than mortals, cannot accomplish? Hunding must be avenged on Siegmund and Sieglinde. Wotan must withdraw his protection from Siegmund. Now appears a phrase which expresses Wotan's impotent wrath—impotent because Fricka brings forward the unanswerable argument that if the Wälsungs go unpunished by her, as guardian of the marriage vow, she, the Queen of the Gods, will be held up to the scorn of mankind.

MOTIVE OF WOTAN'S WRATH.

Wotan would fain save the Wälsungs. But Fricka's argument is conclusive. He cannot protect Siegmund and Sieglinde, because their escape from punishment would bring degradation upon the queen-goddess and the whole race of the gods, and result in their immediate fall. Wotan's wrath rises at the thought of sacrificing his beloved children to the vengeance of Hunding, but he is impotent. His far-reaching plans are brought to nought. He sees the hope of having the Ring restored to the Rhine-daughters by the voluntary act of a hero of the Wälsung race vanish. The curse of Alberich hangs over him like a dark, threatening cloud.

Brünnhilde's joyous shouts are heard from the height. Wotan exclaims that he had summoned the Valkyr to do battle for Siegmund. In broad, stately measures Fricka proclaims that her honour shall be guarded by Brünnhilde's shield and demands of Wotan an oath that in the coming combat the Wälsung shall fall. Wotan takes the oath and throws himself dejectedly down upon a rocky seat. Fricka strides toward the back. She pauses a moment with a gesture of queenly command before Brünnhilde, who has led her horse down the height and into a cave to the right. It will be remembered that in the beginning of this scene Fricka advanced toward Wotan we heard a phrase expressive of sullen dignity. The scene closes with this phrase, but now no longer sullen. It rises in proud beauty like a queenly woman exacting homage.

This is one of those finely artistic touches in which Wagner is peerless.

I have purposely gone somewhat into the details of this scene because it is still so much misunderstood. Yet it is one of Wagner's finest conceptions, and as such it will doubtless be universally ranked at some future day. Aside from the contrast which Fricka, as the champion of virtue, affords to the forbidden revels of the spring night—a contrast of truly dramatic value—we witness the pathetic spectacle of a mighty god vainly struggling to avert ruin from his race. That it is to irresistible fate and not merely to Fricka that Wotan succumbs is made clear by the darkly ominous notes of Alberich's curse, which resound as Wotan, wrapt in gloomy brooding, leans back against the rocky seat, and also when, in a paroxysm of despair, he gives vent to his feelings, a passage which for overpowering intensity of expression stands out even from among Wagner's writings. The final words of this outburst of grief:

"The saddest I among all men,"

are set to this variant of the Motive of Renunciation; the meaning of this phrase having been expanded from the renunciation of love by Alberich to cover the renunciation of happiness which is forced upon Wotan by avenging fate:

Scene II.

Brünnhilde casts away shield, spear and helmet, and sinking down at Wotan's feet, looks up to him with affectionate anxiety. Here we see in the Valkyr the touch of tenderness, without which a truly heroic character is never complete.

Musically, it is beautifully expressed by the Love Motive, which, when Wotan, as if awakening from a reverie, fondly strokes her hair, goes over into the Siegmund Motive. It is over the fate of his beloved Wälsungs Wotan has been brooding. Immediately following Brünnhilde's words:

> "What am I were I not thy will,"

is a wonderfully soft yet rich melody on four horns. It is one of those beautiful details in which Wagner's works abound, yet, although these details are as numerous as they are beautiful, they seem to have escaped the attention of a good many critics. Or have these critics made an effort not to perceive them?

In Wotan's narrative, which now follows, the chief of the gods tells Brünnhilde of the events which have brought this sorrow upon him, of his failure to restore the stolen gold to the Rhine daughters; of his dread of Alberich's curse; how she and her sister Valkyrs were born to him by Erda; of the necessity that a hero should without aid of the gods gain the Ring and Tarnhelmet from Fafner and restore the Rhinegold to the Rhine daughters; how he begot the Wälsungs and inured them to hardships in the hope that one of the race would free the gods from Alberich's curse; of a prophecy uttered by Erda that the end of the gods would be wrought if Alberich could win a woman as wife and beget a son; that Alberich had won a wife and an heir was about to be born to him.

It will have been observed that a considerable portion of Wotan's narrative covers some of the events which were enacted in Rhinegold. Hence a portion of the narrative is unnecessary and therefore undoubtedly faulty from a purely dramatic standpoint. It may also be not unjustly questioned if in other portions the narrative does not go into details beyond the dramatic requirements. Both the scene between Wotan and Fricka and the narrative are too long to be given in their entirety in a performance which begins as late as eight in the evening. When, however, Wagner's works are performed as they are at Bayreuth, where the performances begin at four in the afternoon and there are long intermissions during which the listeners can saunter about the grounds surrounding the theatre, not a note should be omitted. There cannot be under such conditions the faintest suggestion of fatigue from an undue mental strain, even on the part of those who have become so accustomed to the insipidness of the old-fashioned opera that they are appalled at the mere thought—provided they retain the power of thinking—of mental effort in connection with a musico-dramatic work.

Whatever fault may be found with Wotan's narrative—or rather portions of it—from a purely dramatic point of view, it is musically most expressive from its first accents, uttered in a choked, suppressed voice, to its eloquent climax. The motives heard will be recognised, except one, which is new. This is expressive of the stress to which the gods are subjected through Wotan's crime. It is first heard when Wotan tells of the hero who alone can regain the ring. It is the MOTIVE OF THE GODS' STRESS:

Excited by remorse and despair, Wotan bids farewell to the glory of the gods. Then he in terrible mockery blesses the Nibelung's heir. Terrified by this outburst of wrath, Brünnhilde asks what her duty shall be in the approaching combat.

Wotan commands her to do Fricka's bidding and withdraw protection from Siegmund. In vain Brünnhilde pleads for the Wälsung whom she knows Wotan loves, and wished a victor until Fricka exacted a promise from him to avenge Hunding. But her pleading is in vain, Wotan is no longer the all-powerful chief of the gods—through his breach of faith he has become the slave of fate. Hence we hear, as Wotan rushes away, driven by chagrin, rage and despair, chords heavy with the crushing force of fate.

Slowly and sadly Brünnhilde bends down for her weapons, her actions being accompanied by the Valkyr Motive. Bereft of its stormy impetuosity, it is as triste as her thoughts. Lost in sad reflections, which find beautiful expression in the orchestra, she turns toward the background. Suddenly the sadly expressive phrases are interrupted by the Motive of Flight. Looking down into the valley the Valkyr perceives Siegmund and Sieglinde approaching in hasty flight. She then disappears in the cave. With magnificent *crescendo* the Motive of Flight reaches its climax and the two Wälsungs are seen through the natural arch. Sieglinde is hastening in advance of Siegmund. Seeking to restrain her flight, he clasps her tenderly. She stares wildly before her. Her terror of Hunding's pursuit has unsettled her reason. Siegmund speaks to her in gentle tones. Like a reminiscence of happier moments there is heard the wooing, caressing phrase (C) of the love scene in the first act. Sieglinde gazes with growing rapture into Siegmund's eyes and throws her arms around his neck. A fiercely-impassioned phrase accompanies her impetuous action. Then as her mien grows mournful we hear the sadly-reflective version of the Motive of Flight which preceded the Love Motive in the first act. "Away! Away!" she shrieks, suddenly starting up from her reverie.

There is a dramatic change in the music which wildly follows her terrified ejaculations. There is noble calmness and determination in Siegmund's assuring words to her. They are introduced by the Motive of the Wälsung's Fortitude—that eloquent phrase, expressive of the fortitude with which the race has borne the struggle with adverse fate. Here Siegmund proposes to try the steel of his sword with Hunding. Then are heard in the distance the ominous notes of Hunding's horn, summoning his kinsmen to the pursuit of his wife and her lover. Sieglinde starts up in despair. Does not Siegmund hear the avenger's call, bidding the sleuth-hounds join him in the hunt for human prey? An agonising shriek and Sieglinde grows suddenly rigid and stares vacantly before her, as if demented.

Eight chords of terrific force mark the climax of this scene.

In the insanity of her terror she believes that Siegmund is about to desert her, and with a wild cry of despair she throws herself upon his breast. A moment later she hears the distant notes of Hunding's horns, and starts up again in terror. She now believes that Siegmund has deserted her. Her agonised ejaculations, her heartrending grief—these find wonderful, vivid expression. With a furious *crescendo* the climax of the scene is reached, and Sieglinde sinks fainting into Siegmund's arms.

Without releasing his hold upon her, Siegmund lets himself down upon a rocky seat, so that when he assumes a sitting posture her head rests on his lap. Silently he gazes upon her, and then, while the Love Motive whispers of memories of bliss, he presses a kiss upon her brow.

The MOTIVE OF FATE—so full of solemn import—is now heard:

Brünnhilde, leading her horse by the bridle, appears in the entrance of the cave, and advances slowly and solemnly to the front; then pauses and gazes upon Siegmund. While her earnest look rests upon him, there is heard the MOTIVE OF THE DEATH-SONG, a tristly prophetic strain:

Brünnhilde advances and then, pausing again, leans with one hand upon her charger's neck, and grasping shield and spear with the other, gazes upon Siegmund. Then there rises from the orchestra, in strains of rich, soft, alluring beauty, the Valhalla Motive. The Fate, Death-Song and Valhalla Motives recur, and Siegmund, raising his eyes and meeting Brünnhilde's look, questions her and receives her answers. The episode is so fraught with solemnity that the shadow of death seems to have fallen upon the scene. The solemn beauty of the music impresses itself the more upon the listener because of the agitated, agonised scene which preceded it. The alluring pleasures of Valhalla are depicted by the Valhalla Motive, beautifully blended with the Motive of the Valkyrs' Ride, as Brünnhilde announces that many warriors will greet Siegmund's coming: by the Valhalla Motive alone when she tells him that he will meet his father in Valhalla; by the Freia Motive, borne airily upon the buoyant Motive of the Valkyrs' Ride, as she promises him that beauteous wish-maidens will wait upon him in the warrior's heaven.

But these allurements are nought to him. "Shall Siegmund there embrace Sieglinde?" he asks; and when Brünnhilde answers in the negative he spurns the delights she has held out to him. Here he will stand and meet Hunding. Brünnhilde tells him that the sword upon which he relies will be shivered. He draws it to take Sieglinde's life and so pierce the fruit of their love. Moved to admiration by his heroic love, Brünnhilde, in a jubilant outburst, as though a sorrow had been lifted from her heart, proclaims that she will give victory to Siegmund.

Scene III.

When she had disappeared the scene gradually darkens. Heavy storm-clouds veil the crags and hide the peak from view. Siegmund tenderly soliloquises over Sieglinde, and then kissing her gently upon the forehead, disappears among the clouds to meet Hunding. Sieglinde gradually regains her senses. The mountain is now veiled in black thunder-clouds. Hunding's voice is heard summoning Siegmund to combat. She staggers toward the peak. It is suddenly illumined by lightning. In the lurid light the combatants and Brünnhilde hovering above Siegmund are seen. As Siegmund aims a deadly stroke at Hunding a reddish glow diffuses itself through the clouds. In it Wotan appears. He interposes his spear. As the sword strikes it, Siegmund's weapon is shattered and Hunding thrusts his spear into the Wälsung's breast. Sieglinde, with a wild shriek, falls to the ground. Brünnhilde rushes down to her, lifts her upon her steed and urges the charger down the defile. With a gesture of angry contempt Wotan fells Hunding, and then, with a threat to visit upon Brünnhilde dire punishment for her revolt against his will, he disappears amid lightning and thunder. It is impossible in words to do justice to the savage beauty of this closing scene. The music is of the most dramatic character. The warring elements seem to add to the terror of this battle among the clouds. Amid these dark scenes Alberich's second victim finds his death.

Act III.

On the Top of a Rocky Mountain.

Scene I.

The third act opens with the famous ride of the Valkyrs, a number so familiar that detailed reference to it is scarcely necessary. The wild maidens of Valhalla coursing upon winged steeds through storm-clouds, their weapons flashing in the gleam of lightning, their weird laughter mingling with the crash of thunder as they bear slain warriors to the hero's heaven—such is the episode Wagner has depicted with marvellous art. The climax of barbaric joy is reached when the voices of six of the sisters unite in the shout, Hojotoho! Heiaha! When eight of the Valkyrs have gathered upon the rocky summit of the mountain, which is their trysting-place, they see Brünnhilde approaching.

The Motive of the Gods' Stress is the chief theme heard in the ensuing scene when Brünnhilde tells of her disobedience to Wotan and begs the Valkyrs aid her to shield Sieglinde.

The latter, who has been lost in gloomy brooding, starts at her rescuer's supplication and in strains replete with mournful beauty begs that she may be left to her fate and follow Siegmund in death. The glorious prophecy of Brünnhilde, in which she now foretells the birth of Siegfried to Sieglinde, is based upon the SIEGFRIED MOTIVE:

Sieglinde in joyous frenzy blesses Brünnhilde and hastens to find safety in a dense forest to the eastward, the same forest in which Fafner, in the form of a serpent, guards the Rhinegold treasures.

Scene II.

Wotan, in hot pursuit of Brünnhilde, reaches the mountain summit. In vain her sisters entreat him to spare her. He harshly threatens them unless they cease their entreaties, and with wild cries of fear they hastily depart. In the ensuing scene between Wotan and Brünnhilde, in which the latter seeks to justify her action, is heard one of the most beautiful themes of the cycle.

Scene III.

It is the Motive of Brünnhilde's Pleading, which finds its loveliest expression when she addresses Wotan in the passage beginning:

Thou, who this love within my breast inspired.

In the scene there are many passages of rare beauty and many climaxes of great dramatic power. The principal motives employed therein the listener will readily recognise, so that it is only necessary to give in notation the Slumber Motive:

This great scene between Wotan and Brünnhilde is introduced by an orchestral passage. The Valkyr lies in penitence at her father's feet. In the expressive orchestral measures the Motive of Wotan's Wrath mingles with that of Brünnhilde's Pleading. The motives thus form a prelude to the scene in which the Valkyr seeks to appease her father's anger, not through a specious plea, but by laying bare the promptings of a noble heart, which forced her, against the chief god's command, to intervene for Siegmund. The Motive of Brünnhilde's Pleading is heard in its simplest form at Brünnhilde's words:

> Was it so shameful what I have done?

and it may be noticed that as she proceeds the Motive of Wotan's Wrath, heard in the accompaniment, grows less stern until with her plea:

> Soften thy wrath,

it assumes a tone of regretful sorrow.

Wotan's feelings towards Brünnhilde have softened for the time from anger to grief that he must mete out punishment for her disobedience. In his reply excitement subsides to gloom. It would be difficult to point to other music more touchingly expressive of deep contrition than the phrase in which Brünnhilde pleads that Wotan himself taught her to love Siegmund. It is here that the Motive of

Brünnhilde's Pleading assumes the form in the notation given above. Then we hear from Wotan that he had abandoned Siegmund to his fate, because he had lost hope in the cause of the gods and wished to end his woe in the wreck of the world. The weird terror of the Curse Motive hangs over this outburst of despair. In broad and beautiful strains Wotan then depicts Brünnhilde blissfully yielding to her emotions when she intervened for Siegmund.

At last Brünnhilde seeks, with the prophecy of Siegfried, to move Wotan from his purpose, which is to punish her by causing her to fall into a deep sleep and thus become the prey of man. The motive of her pleading, reaching a magnificent climax, passes over to the stately Siegfried Motive as she prays Wotan to surround her sleeping form with horrors which only a true hero will dare strive to overcome. Let him conjure up fire round about her! Wotan raises her to her feet and gazes, overcome with deep emotion, into her eyes. After a majestic orchestral passage there begins Wotan's farewell to Brünnhilde, which in all musico-dramatic numbers for the bass voice has no peer. Such tender, mournful beauty has never found expression in music—and this, whether we regard the vocal part or the orchestral accompaniment in which the Slumber Motive quoted above is prominent. Wotan gently leads Brünnhilde to a table rock, upon which she sinks. He closes her helmet and covers her with her shield. Then, pointing his spear toward a huge rock, he invokes Loge. Tongues of fire leap up from crevices in the rocks. Flickering flames break out on all sides. The forest glows with fire. The magic conflagration—wildly fluttering flames—surrounds Wotan and Brünnhilde. He gazes fondly upon her form and then vanishes among the flames. The Slumber Motive, the Magic Fire Motive and the Siegfried Motive combine to place the music of this scene with the most brilliant and beautiful portion of our heritage from the master-musician. Toward the close of this glorious finale we hear again the ominous muttering of the Motive of Fate. Brünnhilde may be saved from ignominy, Siegfried may be born to Sieglinde—but the crushing weight of the hand of fate rests upon the race of the gods.

"SIEGFRIED."

(SIEGFRIED).

THE Nibelungs were not present in the dramatic action of "The Valkyr," though the sinister influence of Alberich shaped the tragedy of Siegmund's death. In "Siegfried" several characters of "The Rhinegold," who do not take part in "The Valkyr," reappear. These are the Nibelungs Alberich and Mime, the giant Fafner, who, in the guise of a serpent, guards the ring, the tarn-helmet and the Nibelung hoard in a cavern, and Erda. Siegfried has been born of Sieglinde, who died in giving birth to him. This scion of the Wälsung race has been reared by Mime, who is plotting to obtain possession of Fafner's treasures, and hopes to be aided in his designs by the lusty youth. Wotan, disguised as a wanderer, is watching the course of events, again hopeful that a hero of the Wälsung race will free the gods from Alberich's curse. Surrounded by magic fire, Brünnhilde still lies in deep slumber on the rock of the Valkyrs.

ACT I.

A Cave in the Forest.

The vorspiel of Siegfried is expressive of Mime's planning and plotting. It begins with music of a mysterious, brooding character. Mingling with this is the Motive of the Hoard (No. 20), familiar from "The Rhinegold." Then is heard the Nibelung Motive (No. 18), and later, joined with it, the Motive of the Nibelung's Servitude (No. 3). After reaching a forceful climax the Motive of the Nibelung passes over to the Motive of the Ring (No. 6), which rises from *pianissimo* to a crash of tremendous power. The ring is to be the prize of all Mime's plotting, when Siegfried, with a sword of Mime's forging, shall have slain Fafner. The felicitous use of the Sword Motive toward the close of the vorspiel will be readily recognised, as well as the aptness of the Nibelung and Servitude Motives as expressive of Mime's slavish labours, and gaining further point when joined by the Dragon or SERPENT MOTIVE.

The three motives last-named are prominent in the opening scene, which shows Mime forging a sword at a natural forge formed in a rocky cave. In a soliloquy he discloses the purpose of his labours and laments that Siegfried shivers every sword which has been forged for him. Could he (Mime) but unite the pieces of Siegmund's sword! At this thought the Sword Motive rings out brilliantly, and is jubilantly repeated, accompanied by a variant of the Valhalla Motive. For if the pieces of the sword were welded together, and Siegfried were with it to slay Fafner, Mime could surreptitiously obtain possession of the ring, slay Siegfried, rule over the gods in Valhalla and circumvent Alberich's plans for regaining the hoard. This last aspect of Mime's plan is musically expressed by the mocking phrase heard when in "The Rhinegold" Wotan and Loge made sport over the pinioned Alberich. This passage is an admirable example of the wealth of meaning in Wagner's music-drama scores, a meaning perfectly intelligible to anyone who approaches the subject in a serious, studious mood.

Mime is still at work when Siegfried enters, clad in a wild forest garb. Over it a silver horn is slung by a chain. The sturdy youth has captured a bear. He leads it by a bast rope, with which he gives it full play, so that it can make a dash at Mime. As the latter flees terrified behind the forge, Siegfried gives vent to his high spirits in shouts of laughter. Musically his buoyant nature is expressed by a theme inspired by the fresh, joyful spirit of a wild, woodland life. It may be called, to distinguish it from the Siegfried Motive, the MOTIVE OF SIEGFRIED THE FEARLESS:

It pervades with its joyous impetuosity the ensuing scene, in which Siegfried has his sport with Mime, until tiring of it, he loosens the rope from the bear's neck and drives the animal back into the forest. In a pretty, graceful phrase Siegfried tells how he blew his horn, hoping it would be answered by a pleasanter companion than Mime. Then he examines the sword which Mime has been forging. The Siegfried Motive resounds as he inveighs against the weapon's weakness, until, as he shivers the sword on the anvil, the orchestra with a rush takes up the MOTIVE OF SIEGFRIED THE IMPETUOUS:

This is a theme full of youthful snap and dash. It alternates effectively with a contraction of the Nibelung Smithy Motive, while Siegfried angrily scolds Mime, and the latter protests. Finally Mime tells Siegfried how he tenderly reared him from infancy. The music here is as simple and pretty as a folk-song, for Mime's reminiscences of Siegfried's infancy are set to a charming melody, as though Mime were recalling to Siegfried's memory a cradle-song of those days. But Siegfried grows impatient. If Mime tended him so kindly, why should Mime be so repulsive to him; and yet why should he, in spite of Mime's repulsiveness, always return to the cave? The dwarf explains that he is to Siegfried what the father is to the fledgling. This leads to a beautiful lyric episode. Siegfried says that he saw the birds mating, the deer pairing, the she-wolf nursing her cubs. Whom shall *he* call *Mother*? Who is Mime's wife? This episode is pervaded by a lovely, tender motive—the MOTIVE OF LOVE-LIFE:

Mime endeavours to persuade Siegfried that he is his father and mother in one. But Siegfried has noticed that the young of birds and deer and wolves look like the parents. He has seen his features reflected in the brook and knows he does not resemble the hideous Mime. The notes of the Love-Life Motive pervade like woodland strains the musical accompaniment of this episode, in which, when Siegfried speaks of seeing his own likeness, we also hear the Siegfried Motive. The scene which follows is full of mournful beauty. Mime, forced by Siegfried to speak the truth, tells of Sieglinde's death while giving birth to Siegfried. Throughout this scene we find reminiscences of the first act of the Valkyr, the Wälsung Motive, Motive of Sympathy and Love Motive. Finally, when Mime produces as evidence of the truth of his words the two pieces of Siegmund's sword, the Sword Motive rings out brilliantly. Siegfried exclaims that Mime must weld the pieces into a trusty weapon. Here the Motive of Siegfried the Fearless assumes the form in which it is quoted on page 110. The Motive of Siegfried the Impetuous breaks in upon it and the Sword Motive throws its lustre over the music. Then follows Siegfried's Wander Song, so full of joyous abandon. Once the sword welded, he will leave the hated Mime for ever. As the fish darts through the water, as the bird flies so free, he will flee from the repulsive dwarf. With joyous exclamations he runs from the cave into the forest.

In the scenes of which I have just spoken, the

frank, boisterous nature of Siegfried is charmingly portrayed. His buoyant vivacity finds capital expression in the Motives of Siegfried the Fearless, Siegfried the Impetuous and his Wander Song, while the vein of tenderness in his character seems to run through the Love-Life Motive. His harsh treatment of Mime is not brutal; for Siegfried frankly avows his loathing of the dwarf, and we feel, knowing Mime's plotting against the young Wälsung, that Siegfried's hatred is the spontaneous aversion of a frank nature for an insidious one.

After Siegfried has disappeared in the forest, there is a gloomy soliloquy for Mime, interrupted by the entrance of Wotan, disguised as a wanderer. The ensuing scene is one of those lapses from dramatic effectiveness which we find in Wagner, and which surprise us so much, because Wagner was really an inspired dramatist, his works being constructed on fine dramatic lines, the action worked up to fine climaxes and the characters drawn in bold, broad strokes. But occasionally he has committed the error against the laws of dramatic construction of unduly prolonging a scene and thus retarding the dramatic action.

The scene between the Wanderer and Mime covers twenty-seven pages in the Kleinmichel piano score with words, yet it advances us only one step in the dramatic action. As the Wanderer enters, Mime is in despair because he cannot weld the pieces of Siegmund's sword. When the Wanderer departs, he has prophesied that only he who does not know what fear is can weld the fragments, and that through this fearless hero Mime shall lose his life. This prophecy is reached through a somewhat curious process, which must be unintelligible to anyone who has not made a study of the libretto. The Wanderer, seating himself, wagers his head that he can correctly answer any three questions which Mime may put to him. Mime then asks: "What is the race born in the earth's deep bowels?" The Wanderer answers: "The Nibelungs." Mime's second question is: "What race dwells on the earth's back?" The Wanderer replies: "The race of the giants."

Mime finally asks: "What race dwells on cloudy heights?" The Wanderer answers: "The race of the gods." The Wanderer having thus answered correctly Mime's three questions, now puts three questions to Mime: "What is that noble race which Wotan ruthlessly dealt with, and yet which he deemeth most dear?" Mime answers correctly: "The Wälsungs." Then the Wanderer asks: "What sword must Siegfried then strike with, dealing to Fafner death?" Mime answers correctly: "With Siegmund's sword." "Who," asks the Wanderer, "can weld its fragments?" Mime is terrified, for he cannot answer. Then Wotan utters the prophecy of the fearless hero. Whoever will read over this scene will observe that in Wotan's answers the story of "The Rhinegold" is partially retold and that in Mime's answers we have a rehearsal of "The Valkyr." Of course, the narrative repetitions of the plots of preceding music-dramas are undramatic. But I have an idea that Wagner, conjecturing that in many opera-houses his tetralogy would not be given as a whole, and that in some only one or two of the four music-dramas constituting it would be played, purposely introduced these narrative repetitions, in order to familiarise the audience with what preceded the particular music-drama.

But if the scene is dramatically defective it is musically most eloquent. It is introduced by two motives, representing Wotan as the Wanderer. The mysterious chords of the former seem characteristic of WOTAN'S DISGUISE.

The latter, with its plodding, heavily-tramping movement, is the MOTIVE OF WOTAN'S WANDERING.

The third new motive found in this scene is characteristically expressive of the CRINGING MIME.

Several familiar motives from "The Rhinegold" and "The Valkyr" are heard here. The Motive of Compact (No. 9), so powerfully expressive of the binding force of law, the Nibelung (No. 18), Giants' (No. 13) and Valhalla (No. 8) motives from "The Rhinegold," and the Wälsungs's Heroism motives from the first act of "The Valkyr," are among these.

When the Wanderer has vanished in the forest Mime sinks back on his stool in despair. Staring after Wotan into the sunlit forest, the shimmering rays flitting over the soft green mosses with every movement of the branches and each tremor of the leaves seem to him like flickering flames and treacherous will-o'-the-wisps. We hear the Loge Motive (Loge, being the god of fire) familiar from "The Rhinegold" and the finale of "The Valkyr." At last Mime rises to his feet in terror. He seems to see Fafner in his serpent's guise approaching to devour him, and in a paroxysm of fear he falls with a shriek behind the anvil. Just then Siegfried bursts out of the thicket, and with the fresh, buoyant Wander Song and the Motive of Siegfried the Fearless, the weird mystery which hung over the former scene is dispelled. Siegfried looks about him for Mime until he sees the dwarf lying behind the anvil.

Laughingly the young Wälsung asks the dwarf if he has thus been welding the sword. "The sword? The sword?" repeats Mime, confusedly, as he advances, and his mind wanders back to Wotan's prophecy of the fearless hero. Regaining his senses, he tells Siegfried there is one thing he has yet to learn, namely, to be afraid: that his mother charged him (Mime) to teach fear to him (Siegfried). At this point there is heard a combination of the Wälsung Motive and the Nibelung Motive in its contracted form as it previously occurs in this act. Mime asks Siegfried if he has never felt his heart beating when in the gloaming he heard strange sounds and saw weirdly glimmering lights in the forest. Siegfried replies that he never has. He knows not what fear is. If it is necessary before he goes forth in quest of adventure to learn what fear is he would like to be taught. But how can Mime teach him?

The Magic Fire Motive and Brünnhilde's Slumber Motive, familiar from Wotan's Farewell, and the Magic Fire scene in the third act of "The Valkyr" are heard here, the former depicting the weirdly glimmering lights with which Mime has sought to infuse dread in Siegfried's breast, the latter prophesying that, penetrating fearlessly the fiery circle, Siegfried will reach Brünnhilde. Then Mime tells Siegfried of Fafner, thinking thus to strike terror into the young Wälsung's breast. But far from it! Siegfried is incited by Mime's words to meet Fafner in combat. Has Mime welded the fragments of Siegmund's sword, asks Siegfried. The dwarf confesses his impotency. Siegfried seizes the fragments. He will forge his own sword. Here begins the great scene of the forging of the sword. Like a shout of victory the Motive of Siegfried the Fearless rings out and the orchestra fairly glows as Siegfried heaps a great mass of coal on the forge hearth, and, fanning the heat, begins to file away at the fragments of the sword.

The roar of the fire, the sudden intensity of the fierce white heat to which the young Wälsung fans the glow—these we would respectively hear and see were the music given without scenery or action, so graphic is Wagner's score. The Sword Motive leaps like a brilliant tongue of fire over the heavy thuds of a forceful variant of the Motive of Compact, till brightly gleaming runs add to the brilliancy of the score, which reflects all the quickening, quivering effulgence of the scene. How the music flows like a fiery flood and how it hisses as Siegfried pours the molten contents of the crucible into a mould and then plunges the latter into water!

The glowing steel lies on the anvil and Siegfried swings the hammer. With every stroke his joyous excitement is intensified. At last the work is done. He brandishes the sword and with one stroke splits the anvil from top to bottom. With the crash of the Sword Motive, united with the Motive of Siegfried the Fearless, the orchestra dashes into a furious *prestissimo*, and Siegfried, shouting with glee, holds his sword aloft.

Act II.

Depths of the Forest.

The second act opens with a darkly portentous vorspiel. On the very threshold of it we meet Fafner in his motive, which is so clearly based on the Giant Motive that there is no necessity for quoting it. Through themes which are familiar from earlier portions of the work, the vorspiel rises to a crashing *fortissimo*. The curtain lifts on a thick forest. At the back is the entrance to Fafner's cave, the lower part of which is hidden by rising ground in the middle of the stage, which slopes down toward the back. In the darkness the outlines of a figure are dimly discerned. It is the Nibelung Alberich, haunting the domain which hides the treasures of which he was despoiled. The Motive of the Nibelung's Malevolence accompanies his malicious utterances. From the forest comes a gust of wind. A bluish light gleams from the same direction. Wotan, still in the guise of a wanderer, enters.

The ensuing scene between Alberich and the Wanderer is, from a dramatic point of view, episodical. For this and the further reason that the reader will readily recognise the motive occurring in it, detailed consideration of it is unnecessary. Suffice it to say that the fine self-poise of Wotan and the maliciously restless character of Alberich are superbly contrasted. When Wotan has departed the Nibelung slips into a rocky crevice, where he remained hidden when Siegfried and Mime enter. Mime endeavours to awaken dread in Siegfried's heart by describing Fafner's terrible form and powers. But Siegfried's courage is not weakened. On the contrary, with heroic impetuosity, he asks to be at once confronted with Fafner. Mime, well knowing that Fafner will soon awaken and issue from his cave to meet Siegfried in mortal combat, lingers on in the hope that both may fall, until the young Wälsung drives him away.

Now begins the most beautiful lyric episode ever conceived. Siegfried reclines under a linden tree, and looks up through the branches. The rustling of the trees is heard. Over the tremulous whispers of the orchestra—known from concert programmes as the Waldweben (forest-weaving)—rises a lovely variant of the Wälsung Motive. Siegfried is asking himself how his mother may have looked, and this variant of the theme which was first heard in "The Valkyr," when Sieglinde told Siegmund that her home was the home of woe, rises like a memory of her image. Serenely the sweet strains of the Love-Life Motive soothe his sad thoughts. The graceful outlines of the Freia Motive rise for a moment, and then Siegfried, once more entranced by forest sounds, listens intently. Birds' voices greet him. A little feathery songster, whose notes mingle with the rustling leaves of the linden tree, especially charms him.

The forest voices—the humming of insects the piping of the birds, the amorous quiver of the branches—quicken his half-defined aspirations. Can the little singer explain his longing? He listens, but cannot catch the meaning of the song.

Perhaps, if he can imitate it, he may understand it. Springing to a stream hard by, he cuts a reed with his sword, and quickly fashions a pipe from it. He blows on it, but it sounds shrill. He listens again to the bird. He may not be able to imitate its song on the reed, but on his silver horn he can wind a woodland tune. Putting the horn to his lips he makes the forest ring with its notes.*

* The motives are the motive of Siegfried the Fearless and the Siegfried Motive.

The notes of the horn have awakened Fafner who now crawls toward Siegfried. Perhaps the less said about the combat between Siegfried and Fafner the better. This scene, which seems very spirited in the libretto, is ridiculous on the stage. To make it effective it should be carried out very far back—best of all out of sight—so that the magnificent music will not be marred by the sight of an impossible monstrum. The music is highly dramatic. The exultant force of the Motive of Siegmund the Fearless, which rings out like a shout of barbaric joy as Siegfried rushes upon Fafner, the crashing chord as the serpent roars when Siegfried buries the sword in its heart, the rearing, plunging music as the monster rears and plunges with agony—these are some of the most graphic features of the score.*

Siegfried raises his fingers to his lips and licks the blood from them. Immediately after the blood has touched his lips he seems to understand the bird, which has again begun its song, while the forest voices once more weave their tremulous melody. The bird tells Siegfried of the ring and helmet and of the other treasures in Fafner's cave, and Siegfried enters it in quest of them. With his

---

* Observe the significant occurrence of the Motives of the Curse, Siegfried and the Nibelung's Malevolence in the accompaniments to Fafner's dying words.

disappearance the forest weaving suddenly changes to the harsh, scolding notes heard in the beginning of the Nibelheim scene in "The Rhinegold." Mime slinks in and timidly looks about him to make sure of Fafner's death. At the same time Alberich issues forth from the crevice in which he was concealed. This scene, in which the two Nibelungs berate each other after the liveliest fashion is episodical, being hardly necessary to the development of the plot. It is, however, capitally treated, and its humour affords a striking contrast to the preceding scenes.*

As Siegfried comes out of the cave and brings the ring and helmet from darkness to the light of day there are heard the Ring Motive (No. 6), the Motive of the Rhine-daughters' Shout of Triumph (No. 5) and the Rhinegold Motive (No. 4).

These, familiar from "Rhinegold," will be found quoted in the analysis of it. The forest-weaving again begins, and the bird bids the young Wälsung beware of Mime. The dwarf now approaches Siegfried with repulsive sycophancy. But under a smiling face lurks a plotting heart. Siegfried is enabled through the supernatural gifts with which he has become endowed to fathom the purpose of the dwarf, who, unconsciously discloses his scheme

---

* Nibelung and Tarnhelmet Motives are prominent.

to poison Siegfried. The young Wälsung slays Mime, who, as he dies, hears Alberich's mocking laugh. Alberich has felled another victim. Though the Motive of Siegfried the Fearless predominates at this point, we also hear the Nibelung Motive and the Motive of the Curse—indicating the Nibelung's evil intent toward Siegfried.

Siegfried again reclines under the linden. His soul is tremulous with an undefined longing. As he gazes in almost painful emotion up to the branches and asks if the bird can tell him where he can find a friend, his being seems stirred by awakening passion.

The music quickens with an impetuous phrase which seems to define the first joyous thrill of passion in the youthful hero. It is the Motive of Love's Joy (51).

It is interrupted by a beautiful variant of the Motive of Love-Life (No. 47), which continues until above the forest-weaving, the bird again thrills him with its tale of the glorious maid who has so long slumbered upon the fire-guarded rock. With the Motive of Love's Joy coursing through the orchestra, Siegfried bids the feathery songster continue, and, finally, to guide him to Brünnhilde. In answer, the bird flutters from the linden branch, hovers over Siegfried, and hesitatingly flies before him until it takes a definite course toward the background. Siegfried follows the little singer, the MOTIVE OF LOVE'S JOY:

succeeded by that of Siegfried the Fearless, bringing the act to a close.

ACT III.

Wild Region at the Foot of a Rocky Mountain; afterwards: Summit of the Valkyrie's Rock.

The third act opens with a stormy introduction, in which the Motive of the Ride of the Valkyrs (No. 37) accompanies the Motive of the God's Stress (No. 39), the Compact (No. 9) and the Erda Motives (No. 23). The introduction reaches its climax with the MOTIVE OF THE DUSK OF THE GODS (No. 52):

Then to the sombre, questioning phrase of the Motive of Fate, the action begins to disclose the significance of this vorspiel. A wild region at the foot of a rocky mountain is seen. It is night. A fierce storm rages. In dire stress and fearful that through Siegfried and Brünnhilde the rulership of the world may pass from the gods to the human race, Wotan summons Erda from her subterranean dwelling. But Erda has no counsel for the storm-driven, conscience-stricken god. The chief motives which accompany the scene up to this point are familiar from earlier portions of the cycle. They are, besides the Erda and Compact Motives, the Motive of the Dusk of the Gods, the Valhalla and

Fate Motives, and those of the Renunciation, and Brünnhilde's Pleading.

The scene reaches its climax in Wotan's noble renunciation of the empire of the world. Weary of strife, weary of struggling against the decree of fate he renounces his sway. Let the era of human love supplant this dynasty, sweeping away the gods and the Nibelungs in its mighty current. For mournful dignity this episode is unrivalled. It is the last defiance of all-conquering fate by the ruler of a mighty race. After a powerful struggle against irresistible forces, Wotan comprehends that the twilight of the gods will be the dawn of a more glorious epoch. A phrase of great dignity gives force to Wotan's utterances. It is the MOTIVE OF THE WORLD'S HERITAGE:

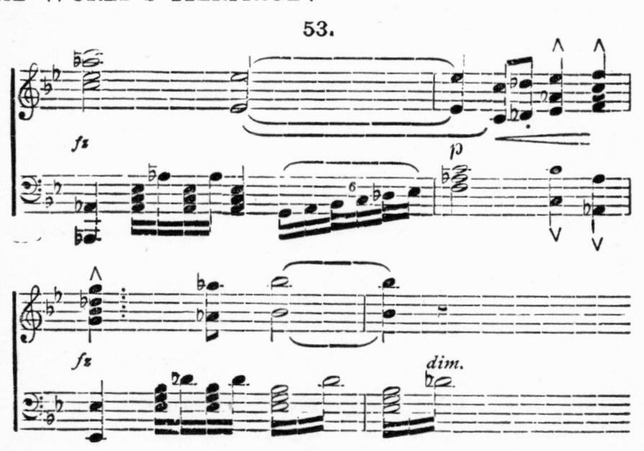

Siegfried enters, guided to the spot by the bird;

Wotan checks his progress with the same spear which shivered Siegmund's sword. Siegfried must fight his way to Brünnhilde. With a mighty blow the young Wälsung shatters the spear and Wotan disappears 'mid the crash of the Motive of Compact—for the spear with which it was the chief of god's duty to enforce compacts is shattered. Meanwhile the gleam of fire has become noticeable. Fiery clouds float down from the mountain. Siegfried stands at the rim of the magic circle. Winding his horn he plunges into the seething flames. Around the Motive of Siegfried the Fearless and the Siegfried Motive flash the Magic Fire and Loge Motives. The Rhine-daughters' Shout of Triumph (No. 5) will be found combined with the Motive of Siegfried the Fearless and there is an interesting sequence of the Siegfried Motive and the Rhine-daughters' Shout of Triumph combined with the Slumber Motive. Siegfried is seen ascending the heights.

The flames having flashed forth with dazzling brilliancy gradually pale before the red glow of dawn till a rosy mist envelopes the scene. When it rises, the Valkyr's Rock and Brünnhilde, in deep slumber under the fir tree, as in the finale of "The Valkyr," are seen. Siegfried appears on the height in the background. As he gazes upon the scene there are heard the Fate and Slumber Motives and then the orchestra weaves a lovely variant of the Freia Motive (No. 12). This is followed by the softly caressing strains of the Fricka Motive (No. 10). Fricka sought to make Wotan faithful to her by bonds of love and hence the Fricka Motive in this scene does not reflect her personality but rather the awakening of the love which is to thrill Siegfried when he has beheld Brünnhilde's features. As he sees Brünnhilde's charger slumbering in the grove, we hear the motive of the Valkyr's Ride, and, when his gaze is attracted by the sheen of Brünnhilde's armour, the theme of Wotan's Farewell. Approaching the armed slumberer under the fir tree Siegfried raises the shield and discloses the figure of the sleeper, the face being almost hidden by the helmet.

He carefully loosens the helmet. As he takes it off, Brünnhilde's face is disclosed and her long curls flow down over her bosom. Siegfried gazes upon her enraptured. Drawing his sword he cuts through the rings of mail on both sides, gently lifts off the corselet and greaves, and Brünnhilde in soft female drapery lies before him. He starts back in wonder. Notes of impassioned import—the Motive of Love's Joy—express the feelings that well up from his heart as for the first time he beholds a woman. The fearless hero is infused with fear by a slumbering woman. The Wälsung Motive, afterwards beautifully varied with the Motive of Love's Joy, accompanies his utterances, the climax of his emotional excitement being expressed in a majestic *crescendo* of the Freia Motive. A sudden feeling of awe gives him at least the outward appearance of calmness. With the Motive of Fate he faces his destiny; and then while the Freia Motive rises like a vision of loveliness, he sinks over Brünnhilde, and with closed eyes presses his lips to hers.

Brünnhilde awakens. Siegfried starts up. She rises and with noble gesture greets in majestic accents her return to the sight of earth. Strains of loftier eloquence than those of her greeting have never been composed. Brünnhilde rises from her magic slumbers in the majesty of womanhood (No. 54).

54.

With the Motive of Fate she asks who is the hero who has awakened her. The superb Siegfried Motive gives back the proud answer. In rapturous phrases they greet one another. It is the MOTIVE OF LOVE'S GREETING (No. 55), which unites their voices in impassioned accents until, as if this motive no longer sufficed to express their ecstasy, it is followed by the MOTIVE OF LOVE'S PASSION (No. 56), which, with the Siegfried Motive, rises and falls with the heaving of Brünnhilde's bosom.

These motives course impetuously through this scene. Here and there we have others recalling former portions of the cycle—the Wälsung Motive, when Brünnhilde refers to Siegfried's mother, Sieglinde; the Motive of Brünnhilde's Pleading, when she tells him of her defiance of Wotan's behest; a variant of the Valhalla Motive, when she speaks of herself in Valhall; and the Motive of the World's Heritage with which Siegfried claims her, this last leading over to a forceful climax of the Motive of Brünnhilde's Pleading, which is followed by a lovely, tranquil episode introduced by the MOTIVE OF LOVE'S PEACE (No. 57), which is succeeded by a motive, ardent yet tender—the MOTIVE OF SIEGFRIED THE PROTECTOR. (No. 58).

These motives accompany the action most expressively. Brünnhilde still hesitates to cast off for ever the supernatural characteristics of the Valkyr

The MOTIVE OF LOVE'S GREETING:

and give herself up entirely to Siegfried. The young hero's growing ecstasy finds expression in the Motive of Love's Joy.

At last it awakens a responsive note of purely human passion in Brünnhilde and, answering the proud Siegfried Motive with the jubilant Shout of

The MOTIVE OF LOVE'S PASSION:

The MOTIVE OF LOVE'S PEACE:

The MOTIVE OF SIEGFRIED THE PROTECTOR:

the Valkyrs and the ecstatic measures of Love's Passion, she proclaims herself his. Then, as river and sea meet in turbulent billows, so meet the emotions of Brünnhilde and Siegfried in a surging flood of music. As she clasps him to her bosom his frame quivers with a joyous thrill, and in a glorious burst of impassioned melody love rises to its rapturous climax. Siegfried and Brünnhilde are united! From the Valkyr, fearful of surrendering her virgin purity lest with it she should lose her goddess-like power, Brünnhilde has changed to a woman, swayed by woman's emotions and passions and with that complete faith in her lover which is perhaps the most .sublime attribute of woman's love.

THE "DUSK OF THE GODS."

(GÖTTERDÄMMERUNG.)

Prelude: On the Valkyrs' Rock.

THE first scene of the prelude is a weirdly effective conference of the three grey sisters of fate—the "Norns" who wind the skein of life. They have met on the Valkyrs' rock and their words forbode the end of the Gods. At last the skein they have been winding breaks—the final catastrophe is impending. The chief motives heard in this scene are the Erda and Fate Motives, with which latter it passes over to the second scene—Siegfried's farewell to Brünnhilde.

An orchestral interlude depicts the transition from the unearthly gloom of the Norn scene to break of day, the climax being reached in a majestic burst of music as Siegfried and Brünnhilde, he in full armour, she leading her steed by the bridle, issue forth from the rocky cavern in the background. The climax owes its sublime eloquence to three motives—that of the Ride of the Valkyrs and two new motives, the one as lovely as the other is heroic, the former being the BRÜNNHILDE MOTIVE (No. 59), the latter the MOTIVE OF SIEGFRIED THE HERO (No. 60):

The Brünnhilde Motive seems to express the strain of pure, tender womanhood in the nature of the former Valkyr. This motive proclaims womanly ecstasy over wholly requited love, as distinguished from the barbaric frenzy of the wild horse-woman of the air, as Brünnhilde appeared to us in the first scene of the second act of "The Valkyr." The Motive of Siegfried the Hero is clearly developed from the Motive of Siegfried the Fearless. The fearless youth has developed into the heroic man. Its outburst from the orchestra in the dawn scene almost simultaneously with the first full effulgence of the day and the forthcoming of Siegfried and Brünnhilde from the cavern recall the psalmist's apostrophe of the sun:

> Which is as a bridegroom coming out of his chamber.

It represents the highest development of manhood. It is the most exaltedly heroic and at the same time, if the expression be allowable, the most muscular motive of the cycle.

In this scene Brünnhilde and Siegfried plight their troth, and Siegfried having given to Brünnhilde the fatal ring and having received from her the steed Grane, which once bore her in her wild course through the storm clouds, bids her farewell and sets forth in quest of further adventure. This scene is one of Wagner's most beautiful creations. In addition to the two new motives already quoted there occurs a third—the MOTIVE OF BRÜNNHILDE'S LOVE (No. 61).

When a woman of a strong, deep nature once gives herself up to love, her passion is as strong and deep as her nature. It is not the surface-heat passion that finds expression in the French drama and the Italian opera to which Wagner has given vent in the music of this scene. It is love rising from the depths of an heroic woman's soul. The grandeur of her ideal of Siegfried, her thoughts of him as a hero winning fame, her pride in his prowess, her love for one whom she deems the bravest among men, find magnificent expression in the MOTIVE OF BRÜNNHILDE'S LOVE:

There also occurs a contracted form of the Motive of Siegfried the Hero which is effectively used throughout the scene, especially in those portions where, after Brünnhilde has given Grane into his charge, it is heard in combination with the Motive of the Ride. This combination of motives is succeeded by a sturdy theme—a bar from Siegfried's wander-song in the first act of "Siegfried," which forms the basis of the impassioned phrases with which Siegfried and Brünnhilde bid one another farewell. Siegfried disappears with the steed behind the rocks and Brünnhilde stands upon the cliff looking down the valley after him; his horn is heard from below and Brünnhilde with rapturous gesture waves him her farewell. The orchestra accompanies the action with the Brünnhilde Motive, the Motive of Siegfried the Fearless, and finally with the theme of the love-duet with which "Siegfried" closed.

The curtain then falls and between the prologue and the first act we have an orchestral interlude descriptive of Siegfried's voyage down the Rhine to the castle of the Gibichungs, where dwell Gunther, his sister Gutrune, and their half-brother Hagen, the son of Alberich. Through Hagen the curse hurled by Alberich in the "Rhinegold" at all into whose possession the ring shall come, is worked out to the end of its fell purpose—Siegfried is betrayed and destroyed and the rule of the gods brought to an end by Brünnhilde's expiation.

In the interlude between the prologue and the first act we first hear the brilliant motive of Siegfried the Fearless and then the gracefully-flowing Motives of the Rhine, and of the Rhine-daughters Shout of Triumph with the Motives of the Rhinegold and Ring. Hagen's malevolent plotting, of which we are so soon to learn in the first act, is foreshadowed by the sombre harmonies which suddenly pervade the music—the Motive of Renunciation and a motive based on that of the Tarnhelmet and expressive of the NIBELUNGS' POWER FOR EVIL:

ACT I.

The Hall of Gunther's Dwelling on the Rhine.
The Valkyrs' Rock.

This act opens in the hall of the Gibichungs, on the Rhine. Gunther, Hagen (Alberich's son) and Gutrune, the sister of Gunther, are plotting against Siegfried, of whose exploit in capturing the ring from Fafner, and freeing Brünnhilde, Hagen knows. Gunther is disposed to be contented with what he has, but Hagen urges him to take a wife and procure a husband for Gutrune, suggesting that she give Siegfried a love-potion, which will excite him to love her and give up Brünnhilde to Gunther.

At the very beginning of this act the Hagen Motive is heard. Particularly noticeable in it are the first two sharp, decisive chords. They recur with frightful force in the third act when Hagen slays Siegfried. The HAGEN MOTIVE is as follows:

This is followed by the GIBICHUNG MOTIVE, the two motives being frequently heard in the opening scene:

Motives prominent in earlier scenes and easily to be recognised occur when Hagen describes the beauty of Brünnhilde and the power of Siegfried, and suggests the infamous trick by which Siegfried is to be induced to win her for Gunther—the Motives of the Ride of the Valkyrs, of the Wälsungs' Heroism, of Siegfried the Fearless, and of the Ring, Renunciation and Gold, followed appropriately by the motive of the Nibelungs' Power through which Siegfried's destruction is to be compassed. Added to these is the MOTIVE OF THE LOVE POTION which is to cause Siegfried to forget Brünnhilde, and conceive a violent passion for Gutrune:

The notes of Siegfried's horn are heard in the distance. As Hagen looks down the river and describes to Gunther how, with an easy stroke, the hero forces the boat against the swift current, we hear an effective combination of the Motives of Siegfried the Fearless (No. 45) and of the Rhine-daughters' Shout of Triumph (No. 5); the Nibelung son's boisterous greeting, in answer to which Siegfried lays to with his boat, is appropriately followed with tragic force by the Motive of the Curse. The Siegfried Motive imparts dignity to the meeting between the young hero and Gunther. When Siegfried asks Hagen how he recognised him although they had never met, the Motive of the Curse (No. 21), prophetically significant, accompanies the query. At the hero's command to Hagen that he heedfully tend Grane, the Brünnhilde Motive (No. 59) and the Motives of Brünnhilde's Love (No. 61), and of the Ride of the Valkyrs (No. 37) are heard. After some parley between the men, Gutrune, who, at a gesture from Hagen, had retired, re-enters bearing a drinking-horn, and approaching Siegfried bids him welcome in the GUTRUNE MOTIVE:

This is followed by the Motive of the Love Potion (No. 65) and then, after the orchestra has murmured memories of the love-scene in "Siegfried," the young hero drains the drinking-horn to Brünnhilde's happiness. His manner suddenly changes. The Motive of the Love Potion becomes more animated. Siegfried regards Gutrune with growing admiration. He asks her of Gunther in marriage.

The Love Potion, which he quaffed to Brünnhilde, has effaced all memory of her. This is made doubly apparent when Gunther asks in return for Gutrune's hand that Siegfried, disguised in the Tarnhelmet as Gunther, penetrate the fiery barrier and lead Brünnhilde as bride to him. Siegfried repeats mechanically, as if endeavouring to collect his thoughts, Gunther's references to the rock and fire, and even the mention of Brünnhilde's name awakens no responsive thrill in him. He offers to bring Brünnhilde to Gunther as bride and to unite himself with the Gibichung by the sacred compact of blood-brotherhood. Each with his sword draws blood from his arm which he allows to mingle with wine in a drinking-horn held by Hagen; each lays two fingers upon the horn, and then, having pledged blood-brotherhood, drinks of the blood and wine. This ceremony is significantly introduced by the Motive of the Curse (No. 21), followed by the Motive of Compact (No. 9). Phrases of Siegfried's and Gunther's pledge are set to a new motive whose forceful simplicity effectively expresses the idea of troth. It is the MOTIVE OF THE VOW:

Abruptly following Siegfried's pledge:

Thus drink I thee troth,

are those two chords of the Hagen Motive which are heard again in the third act when the Nibelung has slain Siegfried.

Gunther and Siegfried enter the latter's boat, cast off and begin their journey to the Valkyr Rock, where Siegfried, under the influence of the magic Love Potion, is to forcibly seize his own bride and deliver her to Gunther. The latter, it should, perhaps, be stated here, is not aware of the union which existed between Brünnhilde and Siegfried, Hagen having carefully concealed this from his half-brother, who hence believes that he will receive the Valkyr in all her goddess-like virginity.

When Siegfried and Gunther have departed, and Gutrune, having sighed her farewell after her lover has retired, Hagen broods with wicked glee over the successful inauguration of his plot. During a brief orchestral interlude a drop curtain conceals the scene which, when the curtain again rises, has changed to the Valkyrs' Rock where sits Brünnhilde lost in contemplation of the Ring, while the Motive of Siegfried the Protector (No. 58) is heard on the orchestra like a blissful memory of the love-scene in "Siegfried."

Her rapturous reminiscences are interrupted by the sounds of an approaching storm, and from the dark cloud there issues one of the Valkyrs, Waltraute, who comes to ask of Brünnhilde that she cast back the ring into the Rhine and thus lift the curse from the race of gods. But Brünnhilde refuses:

> More than Valhalla's welfare,
> More than the good of the gods,
>   The ring I guard.
> From love I part not in life,
> No gods can tear us asunder,
> Soon shall Valhalla's walls
>   Be dust for the winds!

It is dusk. The magic fire rising from the valley throws a glow over the landscape. The notes of Siegfried's horn are heard. Brünnhilde joyously prepares to meet him. Suddenly she sees a stranger leap through the flames. It is Siegfried, who, through the Tarnhelmet (the motive of which, followed by the Gunther motive, dominates the first part of the scene), has assumed the guise of the Gibichung. In vain Brünnhilde seeks to defend herself with the might which the ring imparts. She is powerless against the intruder. As he tears the ring from her finger, the Motive of the Curse (No. 21) resounds with tragic import followed by triste echoes of the Motive of Siegfried the Protector (No. 58) and of the Brünnhilde Motive (No. 59), the last being succeeded by the Tarnhelmet Motive (No. 19), expressive of the evil magic which has wrought this change in Siegfried. Brünnhilde's abject recognition of her impotence is accompanied by the restless, syncopated rhythm of the Nibelungs' Malevolence (No. 22), as she enters the cavern. Before Siegfried follows her he draws his sword Nothung (Needful) and exclaims:

Now Nothung, witness thou, that chaste my wooing is:
To keep my faith with my brother, separate me from his bride.

The music of this closing episode is forcefully graphic. It opens with the abrupt chords of the

Hagen Motive (No. 63). These and the Motive of Compact (No. 9) accompany the Sword Motive (No. 26), when Siegfried draws Nothung. Phrases of the Pledge of Blood-Brotherhood followed by the Brünnhilde, Gutrune and Sword Motives accompany his words. The abrupt Hagen chords lead to the Motives of the Nibelungs' Power and Tarnhelmet which pass into the Brünnhilde Motive. This rises for a moment triumphantly over the sombre, threatening harmonies of malevolence and sorcery. But it ends abruptly; and the chords so forcefully expressive of Hagen's vindictive power, with the Tarnhelmet Motive through which the thuds of the typical Nibelung rhythm resound, lead to the last crashing chord of this eventful act.

ACT II.

In Front of Gunther's Dwelling.

The ominous Motive of the Nibelungs' Hate (No. 22) introduces the second act. The curtain rises upon the exterior of the hall of the Gibichungs. To the right is the open entrance to the hall; to the left the bank of the Rhine, from which rises a rocky ascent toward the background. It is night. Hagen, spear in hand and shield at side, leans in sleep against a pillar of the hall. Through the weird moonlight Alberich appears. He urges

Hagen to murder Siegfried and to seize the ring from his finger. After hearing Hagen's oath that he will be faithful to the hate he has inherited, Alberich disappears. The weirdness of the surroundings, the monotony of Hagen's answers, uttered seemingly in sleep, as if, even when the Nibelung slumbers, his mind remained active, imbue this scene with awful mystery. New in this scene is the MURDER MOTIVE:

A charming orchestral interlude depicts the break of day. Its serene beauty is, however, broken in upon by the MOTIVE OF HAGEN'S WICKED GLEE, which I quote, as it frequently occurs in the course of the succeeding events:

The Motive of Siegfried the Fearless accompanies Siegfried's appearance. When Gutrune joins him and Hagen, and Siegfried relates how he won Brünnhilde for Gunther, the Motive of the Tarnhelmet is frequently heard, usually combined with some other motive. Siegfried having led Gutrune into the hall, Hagen ascends a rocky height and loudly summons the vassals of Gibichung. During the ensuing bustling, noisy scene a variant of the Gutrune Motive is employed as a WEDDING SUMMONS:

A boisterous chorus of rejoicing, barbaric in its sturdy force, greets Gunther as he leads Brünnhilde from the boat to the open space before the hall from which latter Siegfried, Gutrune and her train of women have issued. Soon, however, the shadow if impending tragedy darkens the scene.

When Gunther greets Gutrune and Siegfried with the Motive of the Wedding Summons, Brünnhilde, raising her eyes, perceives Siegfried, on whom her astonished gaze remains riveted. The Motive of Siegfried the Hero, the Sword Motive and the Chords of the Hagen Motive emphasise with a tumultuous crash the dramatic significance of the situation. There is a sudden hush—Brünnhilde astounded and dumb, Siegfried, unconscious of guilt, quietly self-possessed, Gunther, Gutrune and the vassals silent with amazement—it is during this moment of tension that we hear the motive which expresses the thought uppermost in Brünnhilde, the thought which would find expression in a burst of frenzy were not her wrath held in check by her inability to quite grasp the meaning of the situation or to quite fathom the depth of the treachery of which she has been the victim. This is the MOTIVE OF VENGEANCE:

Tenderly the Gutrune Motive, or rather the version of it which formed the Wedding Summons, accompanies Brünnhilde's

> Siegfried here? Gutrune?

and Siegfried's calm response:

> Gunther's mild-eyed sister
> Mate to me as thou to him.

But it is broken in upon by the now unbridled fury of the Motive of Vengeance. Then, again dazed and still incredulous, Brünnhilde totters and is saved from falling only by Siegfried who supports her. Looking up to him as she did when his being thrilled with love of her, she tenderly asks him, while the Brünnhilde Motive adds to the pathos of the scene, if he does not recognise her. Suddenly she sees the ring upon his finger. The crashing chords of the Ring Motive are followed by the Motive of the Curse. Brünnhilde now realises the enormity of Siegfried's treachery—it must have been he, not Gunther, who overcame her. She hurls her accusation at Siegfried with versions of the Motive of Vengeance in which the wrath of injured womanhood seems to attain its most frenzied expression. When she invokes the gods to witness her humiliation the Valhalla Motive is heard. This is followed by the touchingly pathetic Motive of Brünnhilde's Pleading, which, however, soon gives way to the Motive of Vengeance when she calls upon the gods to give her vengeance commensurate with her wrong.

Brünnhilde accuses Siegfried of a threefold crime—of deserting her, of treachery toward Gunther in concealing from him that she had been his (Siegfried's) mate and of wronging Gutrune in wedding her when he had been already mated. Brünnhilde, knowing naught of the love-potion which has caused Siegfried to forget his night of love with her and to conceive a violent passion for Gutrune, thirsts for revenge upon him for his treachery. Her righteous wrath is intensified by jealousy of Gunther's sister, for whom she believes herself to have been deserted. Gunther and Gutrune are also aroused, for Hagen carefully concealed from them all knowledge of the relations between Siegfried and Brünnhilde, and they believe that Siegfried exercised the nuptial privilege the night, when disguised as Gunther, he overcame Brünnhilde —that he has been unfaithful to Gutrune and has broken his vow of Blood-brotherhood with Gunther.

Siegfried takes oath that Brünnhilde's accusation is false; Brünnhilde swears that it is true. The taking of the oath is introduced by the Motive of Vengeance.

Siegfried swears upon Hagen's spear. Hence the fitness of the Murder Motive and of the sharp, decisive chords of the Hagen Motive. As Brünnhilde takes the oath the Valkyr music courses through the orchestra. All her wild Valkyr nature seems unloosed. Siegfried's oath allays Gutrune's suspicions. The tension of the scene is relaxed by the glad measures of the Wedding Summons. Siegfried, throwing his arm round Gutrune, draws her joyously with him into the hall whither they are followed by the vassals and women.

Brünnhilde, Hagen and Gunther remain behind. The Vengeance and Murder Motives and the Motive of the Vow dominate the ensuing scene. Hagen offers to be the executioner of Brünnhilde's and

Gunther's vengeance. Music and action fairly seethe with excitement. In a trio through which fierce, revengeful passions surge, Brünnhilde, Hagen and Gunther swear vengeance upon Siegfried. From this outburst of wrath they turn to behold Gutrune's bridal procession issuing from the hall. The valley of the Rhine re-echoes with glad sounds—but it is the Murder Motive which brings the act to a close.

Act III.

This act plays on the banks of the Rhine, where stands Siegfried baffled in his pursuit of the game. Hagen has arranged that Siegfried shall be slain at a hunt and brought home as if wounded by a boar. While Siegfried stands on the bank of the Rhine, the Rhine-daughters appear to him and promise to bring game in his way if he will give them the ring. He refuses and they disappear, leaving him to his fate. For charming badinage this scene can be compared only with the opening scene in "The Rhinegold." The ripples of a lovely river do not exceed in grace the music with which Wagner has adorned this episode.

Distant hunting horns are heard. Gunther, Hagen and their attendants gradually assemble and encamp themselves. Hagen fills a drinking-horn and hands it to Siegfried, whom he persuades to relate the story of his life. This Siegfried does in a wonderfully picturesque, musical and dramatic story in which motives, often heard before, charm us anew.*

In the course of the narrative he refreshes himself by a draught from the drinking-horn into which meanwhile Hagen has pressed the juice of a herb. Through this the effect of the Love-Potion is so far counteracted that tender memories of Brünnhilde well up within him and he tells with artless enthusiasm how he won her. Gunther springs up aghast at this revelation. Now he knows that Brünnhilde's accusation was true.

Two ravens fly overhead. As Siegfried turns to look after them the Motive of the Curse resounds and Hagen plunges his spear into the young hero's back. Gunther and the vassals throw themselves upon Hagen. The Siegfried Motive, cut short with a crashing chord, the two murderous chords of the Hagen Motive forming the bass—and Siegfried, who with a last effort has heaved his shield aloft to hurl it at Hagen, lets it fall and, collapsing, drops upon it. So overpowered are the witnesses by the suddenness and enormity of the crime that after a few disjointed exclamations, they gather,

---

* Nibelung, Sword, Dragon, Forest-weaving, Tarnhelmet, Brünnhilde's Love, Brünnhilde, Magic Fire and Brünnhilde's Greeting.

bowed with grief, around Siegfried, Hagen with stony indifference turns away and disappears over the height.

With the fall of the last scion of the Wälsung race we hear a new motive, simple yet indescribably fraught with woe—the DEATH MOTIVE.

Siegfried supported by two men rises to a sitting posture and with a strange rapture gleaming in his glance intones his death-song. It is an ecstatic greeting to Brünnhilde. "Brünnhilde!" he exclaims, "thy wakener comes to wake thee with his kiss." The ethereal harmonies of the Motive of Brünnhilde's Awakening, the Motive of Fate, the Siegfried Motive swelling into the Motive of Love's Greeting and dying away through the Motive of Love's Passion to Siegfried's last whispered accents —"Brünnhilde beckons to me"—in the Motive of Fate—and Siegfried sinks back in death.

Full of pathos though this episode be, it but brings us to the threshold of a scene of such overwhelming power that it may without exaggeration be singled out as the supreme musical-dramatic effect in all that Wagner wrought, and hence the supreme effect in all music. Siegfried's last ecstatic greeting to his Valkyr bride has made us realise the blackness of the treachery which tore the young hero and Brünnhilde asunder and led to his death; and now as we are bowed down with a grief too deep for utterance—like the grief with which a nation gathers at the grave of its noblest hero—Wagner voices for us in music of overwhelmingly tragic power feelings which are beyond expression in human speech. This is not a funeral march, as it is often absurdly called—it is the awful mystery of death itself expressed in music.

Motionless with grief, the men gather around Siegfried's corpse. Night falls. The moon casts a pale, sad light over the scene. At the silent bidding of Gunther, the vassals raise the body and bear it in solemn procession over the rocky height. Meanwhile with majestic solemnity the orchestra voices the funeral oration of the "world's greatest hero." One by one, but tragically interrupted by the Motive of Death, we hear the motives which tell the story of the Wälsungs' futile struggle with destiny—the Wälsung Motive, the Motive of the Wälsung's Heroism, the Motive of Sympathy and the Love Motive, the Sword Motive, the Siegfried Motive and the Motive of Siegfried the Hero, around which the Death Motive swirls and crashes like a black, death-dealing, all-wrecking flood, forming an overwhelmingly powerful climax that dies away into the Brünnhilde Motive, with which, as with a heartbroken sigh, the heroic dirge is brought to a close.

Meanwhile the scene has changed to the hall of

the Gibichungs, as in the first act. Gutrune is listening through the night for some sound which may announce the return of the hunt.

Men and women bearing torches precede in great agitation the funeral train. Hagen grimly announces to Gutrune that Siegfried is dead. Wild with grief, she overwhelms Gunther with violent accusations. He points to Hagen, whose sole reply is to demand the ring as spoil. Gunther refuses. Hagen draws his sword and after a brief combat slays Gunther. The victorious Nibelung is about to snatch the ring from Siegfried's finger, when the corpses's hand suddenly raises itself threateningly, and all—even Hagen—fall back in consternation.

Brünnhilde advances solemnly from the back. While watching on the bank of the Rhine she has learned from the Rhine-daughters the treachery of which she and Siegfried have been the victims. Her mien is ennobled by a look of tragic exaltation. To her the grief of Gutrune is but the whining of a child. When the latter realises that it was Brünnhilde whom she caused Siegfried to forget through the love-potion, she falls fainting over Gunther's body. Hagen leaning on his spear is lost in gloomy brooding.

Brünnhilde turns solemnly to the men and women and bids them erect a funeral pyre. The orchestral harmonies shimmer with the Magic Fire Motive through which courses the Motive of the Ride of the Valkyrs. Then, her countenance transfigured by love, she gazes upon her dead hero and apostrophises his memory in the Motive of Love's Greeting. From him she looks upward and in the Valhalla Motive and the Motive of Brünnhilde's Pleading, passionately inveighs against the injustice of the gods. The Curse Motive is followed by a wonderfully beautiful combination of the Valhalla Motive and the Motive of the God's Stress at Brünnhilde's words:

Rest thee! Rest thee! O God!

For, with the fading away of Valhalla, and the inauguration of the reign of human love in place of that of lust and greed—a change to be wrought by the approaching expiation of Brünnhilde for the crimes which began with the wresting of the Rhinegold from the Rhine-daughters—Wotan's stress will be at an end. Brünnhilde having told in the graceful, rippling Rhine music how she learned of Hagen's treachery through the Rhine-daughters, places upon her finger the ring. Then turning toward the pyre upon which Siegfried's body rests, she snatches a huge fire-brand from one of the men. Flinging it upon the pyre, which kindles brightly, she hurries toward Grane. As the moment of her immolation approaches, the Motive of Expiation begins to dominate the scene.

It wings its flight higher and higher until it seems to have soared to the height of emotional exaltation. Brünnhilde swings herself upon Grane's back, and with a mighty bound the steed bears his noble rider into the blazing pyre. Men and women in extreme terror crowd into the foreground. Suddenly the Rhine is seen to overflow, and borne on the flood the Rhine-daughters swim to the pyre and reclaim the ring. Hagen plunges madly after them into the flood and they draw him down with them. A deep glow illumines the heavens. It is the dusk of the gods. Valhalla is seen enveloped in flames. Once more the Valhalla Motive resounds majestically. But the Motive of Expiation breaks in upon it with overwhelming power. For the last time we hear the Siegfried Motive and then with the Motive of Expiation a new era—that of human love—rises in all its glory from the ruins of the empire of the gods.

THE END.

Printed by The New Temple Press, Norbury Crescent, S.W.

CATALOGUE OF BOOKS ON MUSIC

Literature covering every branch of Music, Biographical and Critical Studies of Composers, Histories of Musical Instruments, also valuable Textbooks and Tutors for Teachers and Students of the Piano, Organ, Violin, Cello, Theory, Singing, etc.

All prices are net and postage extra

Published by

WILLIAM REEVES Bookseller Limited

1a Norbury Crescent, London, S.W.16

Telephone: POLlards 2108

ÆSTHETICS, CRITICISMS, ESSAYS

PAN PIPES, THE SPIRIT OF MUSIC in Nature, Art and Legends, from East to West. Sixteen Articles for General Reading, with Drawings of Eastern Musical Instruments. By G. P. GREEN. Crown 8vo, cloth, 7/6.

HOW TO LISTEN TO GOOD MUSIC and Encourage the Taste in Instrumental and Vocal Music. With many useful Notes for Listener and Executant. By K. BROADLEY GREENE. Complete, cloth, 6/–, or in two books, paper, 2/6 each.

SOME FAMOUS SYMPHONIES, How to Understand Them. With their Story and Simple Analysis. Numerous Portraits. By J. F. PORTE. Dealing with Symphonies of Beethoven, Berlioz, Borodin, Brahms, Chausson, Dvorák, Elgar, César Franck, Haydn, Mendelssohn, Mozart, Schubert, Stanford and Tchaïkovsky. Complete in cloth, 8/–, or in 2 separate parts, paper, 2/6 each.

THE DEATH AND RESURRECTION OF THE MUSICAL FESTIVAL. By RUTLAND BOUGHTON. 8vo, paper covers, 2/–.

The Decay of Triennials—The Rise of Competitions—The Reform of Competitions—The Festival of the Future.

SOME ASPECTS OF CHINESE MUSIC AND SOME THOUGHTS AND IMPRESSIONS ON ART PRINCIPLES IN MUSIC. By G. P. GREEN. Post 8vo, cloth, 6/–, paper covers, 3/6.

THE FUTURE OF MUSIC. Coming Changes Outlined in Regard to Composer, Conductor and Orchestra. By LOUIS LALOY. Translated by MRS. FRANZ LIEBICH. 8vo, cloth, 3/6, paper, 2/–.

SOME ASPECTS OF GIPSY MUSIC. By D. C. PARKER. Post 8vo, cloth, 6/–, paper covers, 3/6.

MUSIC AND MUSICIANS. Essays and Criticisms, by ROBERT SCHUMANN. Translated, Edited and Annotated by F. R. RITTER. Two volumes, crown 8vo, cloth, 21/– each.

Schumann's literary gifts and interests almost equalled his musical ones. From boyhood he was drawn to literary expression, and his writings on music belong to the best among the romantic literature of the 19th century. The same fire, poetry, directness of expression, the same inventiveness we love in his compositions, also animates his prose.

THE DEEPER SOURCES OF THE BEAUTY AND EXPRESSION OF MUSIC. By JOSEPH GODDARD. With many Musical Examples. Crown 8vo, cloth, 7/6.

WOMAN AS A MUSICIAN. An Art Historical Study. By F. R. RITTER. 8vo, 3/–.

MUSICAL DEVELOPMENT, or Remarks on the Spirit of the Principal Musical Forms. An Æsthetical Investigation, in which an Attempt is made to show the Action in Music of certain Laws of Human Expression; to point out what are the Spiritual Aims of the Chief Forms of Composition, and the Broad Principles upon which they should be Constructed. By JOSEPH GODDARD. 8vo, cloth, 10/–.

IN THE SERVICE OF ART. A plea for Simplicity in Music. By J.-JOACHIM NIN. Translated by MRS. FRANZ LIEBICH. Post 8vo, 2/6.

THE PLACE OF SCIENCE IN MUSIC. By H. SAINT-GEORGE. For Advanced Students of Harmony. With music examples. 8vo, 2/6.

NECESSITY OF MUSIC IN THE SCHOOL CURRICULUM. Address delivered to Members of the Music Teachers' Association. By A. W. POLLITT, *Mus.D., F.R.C.O.* 8vo, 1/6.

ÆSTHETICS OF MUSICAL ART, or The Beautiful in Music. By DR. FERDINAND HAND. Translated from the German by WALTER E. LAWSON, *Mus.Bac. Cantab, etc.* Third Edition. Crown 8vo, cloth, 10/–.

NATIONAL SCHOOL OF OPERA FOR ENGLAND. Being the Substance of a Paper read at Trinity College, London. By FRANK AUSTIN. 1/–.

MUSIC IN THE HIRSCH LIBRARY (Part 53 of the Catalogue of Printed Music in the British Museum), by A. HYATT KING and C. HUMPHRIES, 1951. Published for the Trustees of the British Museum. This catalogue, prepared by the Museum staff, lists also a considerable number of works which were either not included in the original four volume catalogue by P. Hirsch, or were acquired later. 4to, cloth, 42/–.

BOOKS ABOUT MUSICIANS AND THEIR WORKS

I.—COLLECTED

STUDIES IN RUSSIAN MUSIC. Critical Essays on the most important of Rimsky-Korsakov's operas, Borodin's "Prince Igor," Dargomïzhsky's "Stone Guest," etc.; with chapters on Glinka, Mussorgsky, Balakirev and Tschaïkovsky. By GERALD ABRAHAM. 92 music examples. 350 pages, demy 8vo, cloth, 25/–.

ON RUSSIAN MUSIC. Critical and Historical Studies of Glinka's Operas, Balakirev's Works, etc. With chapters dealing with Compositions by Borodin, Rimsky-Korsakov, Tchaïkovsky, Mussorgsky, Glazunov, and various other Aspects of Russian Music. By GERALD ABRAHAM. With Frontispiece and 88 Music Examples. Demy 8vo, cloth, 21/–.

The above two books complement one another, and together form a valuable survey of Russian music of the period 1836 to 1910. The operas of Rimsky-Korsakov are studied fully, also Borodin's "Prince Igor", Glinka's operas and Balakirev's music. Gerald Abraham is Professor of Music at Liverpool University, and is the chief English authority on Russian music.

FROM MENDELSSOHN TO WAGNER. Being the Memoirs of J. W. Davison, forty years Music Critic of *The Times*, compiled by his son, HENRY DAVISON, from Memoranda and Documents. With 52 portraits of Musicians and Important Letters (previously unpublished) of Mendelssohn, Berlioz, Gounod, Jullien, Macfarren, Sterndale Bennett, etc. Index, 539 pages, 8vo, cloth, 35/–.

WITH THE GREAT COMPOSERS. A Series of Pen Pictures, exhibiting in the form of Interviews the Personal Characteristics as Artists of the World's great Tone Poets. By GERALD CUMBERLAND. Portraits. Cr. 8vo, cloth, 10/–.

Deals with Chopin, Haydn, Mendelssohn, Paganini, Beethoven, Handel, Rossini, Schubert, Liszt, Berlioz, Mozart, Wagner Tchaïkovsky, Cherubini, Wolf, Borodin, Schumann, Sullivan.

THE SYMPHONY WRITERS SINCE BEETHOVEN. Critical Essays on Schubert, Schumann, Götz, Brahms, Tchaïkovsky, Brückner, Berlioz, Liszt, Strauss, Mahler, Mendelssohn, Saint-Saëns, etc. By FELIX WEINGARTNER. Translated by A. BLES. Twelve Portraits. *Second Impression.* With Chapter added by D. C. PARKER on Weingartner's Symphony No. 5. Crown 8vo, cloth, 12/6.

REEVES' DICTIONARY OF MUSICIANS. Biographical Accounts of about 2,500 Noteworthy Musicians of the Past and Present. Edited by EDMUNDSTOUNE DUNCAN and Others. Crown 8vo, cloth, 7/6, paper covers, 4/–.

SKETCHES OF GREAT PIANISTS AND GREAT VIOLINISTS. Biographical and Anecdotal, with Account of the Violin and Early Violinists. Viotti, Spohr, Paganini, De Beriot, Ole Bull, Clementi, Moscheles, Schumann (Robert and Clara), Chopin, Thalberg, Gottschalk, Liszt. By G. T. FERRIS. Third Edition. Crown 8vo, cloth, 8/6.

SKETCHES OF ENGLISH GLEE COMPOSERS. Historical, Biographical and Critical. From about 1735–1866. By D. BAPTIE. Post 8vo, cloth, 8/6.

ENGLISH GLEE AND MADRIGAL WRITERS. By W. A. BARRETT. 8vo, paper covers, 5/–.

SOME MUSICAL RECOLLECTIONS OF FIFTY YEARS. By RICHARD HOFFMAN. With Memoir by MRS. HOFFMAN. Illustrated with many Portraits. Crown 8vo, cloth, 10/–.

An interesting book of reminiscences by a prominent Anglo-American pianist and composer (1831–1909). He studied under Pleyel, Moscheles, Rubinstein and Liszt, and became a concert pianist in New York, and also toured with Jenny Lind. Hoffman composed and published many pianoforte pieces of the brilliant kind in vogue at the time.

MUSICAL MEMORIES. By WILLIAM SPARK, *Mus.Doc.* (*late Organist of the Town Hall, Leeds*). Third Edition. With sixteen Portraits. Thick crown 8vo, cloth, 10/–.

BIOGRAPHICAL DICTIONARY OF FIDDLERS. Including Performers on the Violoncello and Double Bass, Past and Present. Containing a Sketch of their Artistic Career, together with Notes of their Compositions. By A. MASON CLARKE. Nine Portraits. Post 8vo, cloth, 10/–.

HOW TO STUDY THE PIANOFORTE WORKS OF THE GREAT COMPOSERS. By HERBERT WESTERBY, *Mus.Bac.* Handel, Bach, Haydn, Scarlatti, Mozart, Clementi, C. P. E. Bach, Beethoven. With 123 Musical Examples. Crown 8vo, cloth, 12/6.

The following issued singly, paper covers:
HANDEL, 1/–; D. SCARLATTI, 1/–; J. S. BACH, 1/6; C. P. E. BACH AND HAYDN, 1/–; CLEMENTI, 1/–; MOZART, 1/6.

BRITISH MUSICAL BIOGRAPHY. A Dictionary of Musical Artists, Authors and Composers born in Britain and its Colonies. By J. D. BROWN and S. S. STRATTON. 8vo, cloth, 21/–.

Despite its age, this book is still of importance because it contains particulars of many musicians not listed elsewhere.

THE CRITICAL WRITINGS OF HECTOR BERLIOZ

A CRITICAL STUDY OF BEETHOVEN'S NINE SYMPHONIES, with a few Words on his Trios and Sonatas, and a Criticism of Fidelio. Portrait. Crown 8vo, cloth, 21/–.

GLUCK AND HIS OPERAS, with an Account of their Relation to Musical Art. Portrait. Crown 8vo, cloth, 18/–.

MOZART, WEBER AND WAGNER, with various other Essays on Musical Subjects. Crown 8vo, cloth, 18/–.

The above three books form a full and readable translation by Edwin Evans of the justly celebrated critical writings of Hector Berlioz issued under the title of "A Travers Chant."

BOOKS ABOUT MUSICIANS AND THEIR WORKS

II.—INDIVIDUAL.

HOW TO PLAY BACH'S 48 PRELUDES AND FUGUES. A Guide Book for the use of Piano Students as an aid to the Unravelling and Interpretation of these Masterpieces, ensuring a more Intelligent Keyboard Rendering. By C. W. WILKINSON. Crown 8vo, cloth, 10/-.

THE FORTY-EIGHT FUGUES IN THE WELL-TEMPERED CLAVIER (Das Wohltemperirte Klavier). By J S. BACH. Analysed by BROOK SAMPSON, *Mus.Bac. Oxon., F.R.C.O.* Following obtainable, 1/6 *each.*

No. 4, in C. sharp minor
No. 9, in E major
No. 16, in G minor
No. 18, in G sharp minor
No. 24, in B minor
No. 28, in C sharp minor
No. 29, in D major
No. 34, in E minor
No. 36, in F minor
No. 38, in F sharp minor
No. 40, in G minor

OUTLINE ANALYSIS OF BACH'S FORTY-EIGHT FUGUES. By BROOK SAMPSON. 3/-.

BALFE, HIS LIFE AND WORK. By WM. ALEXANDER BARRETT. Over 300 pages. Crown 8vo, cloth, 12/6.

A CRITICAL STUDY OF BEETHOVEN'S NINE SYMPHONIES, with a Few Words on His Trios and Sonatas, a Criticism of "Fidelio" and an Introductory Essay on Music. By HECTOR BERLIOZ. Translated from the French by EDWIN EVANS. Portrait. Crown 8vo, cloth, 21/-.

BEETHOVEN AND HIS PIANO WORKS (Sonatas, Concertos, Variations, etc.). Descriptive and Analytic Aid to their Understanding and Rendering. By HERBERT WESTERBY. With list of Principal Editions and Bibliography. 3 illustrations, 45 music examples. Crown 8vo, cloth, 10/-.

BEETHOVEN'S PIANOFORTE SONATAS Explained for the Lovers of the Musical Art. By ERNST VON ELTERLEIN. Translated by E. HILL, with Preface by ERNST PAUER. Revised Edition (the Seventh issue). With Portrait, and View of Beethoven's House. Crown 8vo, cloth, 10/-.

"He writes with the ripe knowledge and thorough understanding of a practical musician. Every musical student or amateur can safely trust him as a competent and agreeable guide."—E. PAUER.

BEETHOVEN'S NINE SYMPHONIES Fully Described and Analysed. A complete Account of Thematic Material and auxiliary Motives, an Analytical Chart of each Movement, full Technical Descriptions of Developments, Particulars of Formal and Rhythmic Features, Epitomical Tables, etc. Illustrated by 637 Musical Examples. By EDWIN EVANS. Cloth, Vol. I (Nos. 1 to 5), 21/–. Vol. II (Nos. 6 to 9), out of print.

BEETHOVEN'S SYMPHONIES in their Ideal Significance, Explained by ERNST VON ELTERLEIN. Translated by FRANCIS WEBER. With an Account of the Facts Relating to Beethoven's Tenth Symphony. By L. NOHL. Second Edition. Crown 8vo, cloth, 10/–.

BEETHOVEN'S SYMPHONIES Critically Discussed by ALEXANDER TEETGEN. With Preface by JOHN BROADHOUSE. Second Edition. Post 8vo, cloth, 6/6.

BEETHOVEN'S PIANO SONATAS. A Descriptive Commentary on the Sonatas in the light of Schnabel's Interpretations; giving an æsthetic Appreciation of each Sonata, with an Outline of the Development of the Sonata Form in Beethoven's hands. With a Biographical Sketch of Schnabel and an account of his activity as an executant, composer and teacher. By RUDOLF KASTNER. Translated by GERALD ABRAHAM. 55 pages, post 8vo, paper, 3/6.

NOTES ON THE INTERPRETATION OF 24 FAMOUS PIANO SONATAS BY BEETHOVEN. By J. ALFRED JOHNSTONE. Portrait, crown 8vo, cloth, 12/6.

BEETHOVEN. By RICHARD WAGNER. With a Supplement from the Philosophical Works of Arthur Schopenhauer. Translated by EDWARD DANNREUTHER. Third Edition. Crown 8vo, cloth, 15/–.

"It is a plain duty to be familiar and even intimate with the opinion of one famous man about another. Gladly therefore we welcome Mr. Dannreuther's translation of the work before us. Mr. Dannreuther has achieved his task with the conscientiousness of his nature and with a success due to much tact and patience."—*Musical Times.*

"This work contains his contributions towards the metaphysics of music, if, indeed such can be said to exist. Apart, however, from metaphysics, the work is an exposition of Wagner's thoughts on the significance of Beethoven's music."—*Grove's Dictionary.*

BORODIN THE COMPOSER AND HIS MUSIC. A Descriptive and Critical Analysis of his Works and a Study of his Value as an Art Force. With many references to the Russian Kouchka Circle of Five—Balakirev, Moussorgsky, César Cui, Rimsky-Korsakov, and Borodin. By GERALD ABRAHAM. With music examples and 5 Portraits. Crown 8vo, cloth, 18/–.

LIFE OF JOHANNES BRAHMS. By FLORENCE MAY. Second Edition, Revised. Two Volumes, demy 8vo, cloth, 35/–.

This work still remains the most comprehensive single work on the composer published. It is based on material gathered at first hand during the course of several visits to the Continent, and its value as a personal document is enhanced by the author's own recollections and impressions of Brahms, which were the result of personal contact with and actual study under the great master.

HISTORICAL, DESCRIPTIVE AND ANALYTICAL ACCOUNT OF THE ENTIRE WORKS OF BRAHMS. By EDWIN EVANS. The Works are treated in the order of their Opus Numbers, and every Composition is dealt with in detail. Complete in 4 volumes with altogether 1,500 pages and over 1,000 Music Examples and Tables, as follows:

CHAMBER AND ORCHESTRAL WORKS OF BRAHMS. First Series to Op. 67. By EDWIN EVANS. 30/–.

CHAMBER AND ORCHESTRAL WORKS OF BRAHMS. Second Series, Op. 68 to the End. By EDWIN EVANS. 30/–.

PIANO AND ORGAN WORKS OF BRAHMS. By EDWIN EVANS. 30/–.

VOCAL WORKS OF BRAHMS. By EDWIN EVANS. 35/–.

CHOPIN, HIS LIFE AND LETTERS. By MORITZ KARASOWSKI. Translated by EMILY HILL. Third Edition, with additional Letters in Polish with English translation, Chopin to Grzymala, and extra Illustrations. Fourteen Illustrations. Crown 8vo, cloth, 42/–.

Karasowski was a close friend of the family of Chopin and was intimate with them for several years. He was given access to the letters, many of which were subsequently destroyed during the Warsaw insurrection, written by Chopin to his family in Poland throughout his life abroad. These facts give this work particular value, and to it we are also indebted for valuable information regarding Chopin's life.

CHOPIN'S GREATER WORKS (Preludes, Ballads, Nocturnes, Polonaises, Mazurkas). How they should be Understood. By J. KLECZYNSKI. Including Chopin's Notes for a "Method of Methods." Translated by N. JANOTHA. Second Edition. With music examples. Crown 8vo, cloth, 8/6.

HOW TO PLAY CHOPIN. The Works of Chopin, their Proper Interpretation. By J. KLECZYNSKI. Translated by A. WHITTINGHAM. Sixth Edition. Music Illustrations. Crown 8vo, cloth, 7/6.

Contains the cream of Chopin's instructions to his own pupils. To admirers of Chopin and players of his music we should say this book is indispensable.

FREDERIC CHOPIN, Critical and Appreciative Essay. By J. W. DAVISON. 8vo, 3/–.

CHOPIN AS REVEALED BY EXTRACTS FROM HIS DIARY. By COUNT TARNOWSKI. Translated from the Polish by N. JANOTHA. With eight Portraits. Crown 8vo, paper covers, 5/–.

In the above notes Chopin alludes to many of his compositions as well as relating the conditions under which they were written.

CHOPIN THE COMPOSER AND HIS MUSIC. An Analytic Critique of Famous Traditions and Interpretations, as exhibited in the Playing of Great Pianists, Past and Present. By JOHN F. PORTE. With portrait. 193 pages, crown 8vo, cloth, 10/6.

"Your excellent book gives me supreme pleasure. You judge tradition so well. I thank you for your artistic sympathy and your wonderful book."—MORITZ ROSENTHAL.

HANDBOOK TO CHOPIN'S WORKS. A Detailed Account of all the Compositions of Chopin. Short Analyses for Piano Student and Critical Quotations from Writings of Well-known Musical Authors. Chronological List of Works, etc. By G. C. A. JONSON. Second Edition. Crown 8vo, cloth, 18/–.

"Here in one compact volume is all that is necessary to know about Chopin and his works except by the leisured enthusiast."

LIFE OF CHERUBINI. By F. J. CROWEST. (Great Musicians Series.) Crown 8vo, cloth, 6/–.

CHERUBINI. Memorials illustrative of his life. By E. BELLASIS. Crown 8vo, cloth, 21/–.

GLUCK AND HIS OPERAS. With an Account of their Relation to Musical Art. By HECTOR BERLIOZ. Translated from the French by EDWIN EVANS. Portrait. Crown 8vo, cloth, 18/–.

HANDEL'S MESSIAH. The Oratorio and its History. A Handbook of Hints and Aids to its Public Performance, with useful Notes on each Movement, as well as Numerous References and much Original Information. By J. ALLANSON BENSON. Cloth, 6/–, paper, 3/–.

LISZT, COMPOSER, AND HIS PIANO WORKS. Descriptive Guide and Critical Analysis, written in a popular and concise style. By HERBERT WESTERBY, *Mus.Bac., Lon., etc.* 5 illustrations, 24 music examples. 336 pp., crown 8vo, cloth, 12/6.

HOW TO INTERPRET MENDELSSOHN'S "SONGS WITHOUT WORDS" (the celebrated "Lieder ohne Worte"). A Readable and Useful Guide for All. Gives the Piano Students helpful Insight into the first Principles of Form in Music. By CHARLES W. WISKINSON. With portrait and facsimile of MS. Crown 8vo, cloth, 6/–; paper, 3/6.

These notes on each of the "Lieder" will help the student in playing these homely and easily intelligible compositions.

ANALYSIS OF MENDELSSOHN'S ORGAN WORKS. A Study of their Structural Features. By JOSEPH W. G. HATHAWAY, *Mus.B. Oxon.* 127 Music Examples. Portrait and Facsimiles. Crown 8vo, cloth, 10/–.

MOZART: a Commemorative Address read before the Positivist Society. By V. LUSHINGTON. 8vo, 2/–.

Mozart and Religion.

MOZART AND THE SONATA FORM: A Companion Book to any Edition of Mozart's Piano Sonatas, including an Analysis of the Form of each Movement, with Notes upon Treatment and Tonality, by J. RAYMOND TOBIN, *Mus.B.* Crown 8vo, cloth, 12/–.

THE SONATA: Its Form and Meaning, as Exemplified in the Piano Sonatas by Mozart. A Descriptive Analysis, with Musical Examples. By F. HELENA MARKS. 8vo, cloth, 16/–.

QUESTIONS ON MOZART'S SONATAS. By F. HELENA MARKS. Aid and Companion to the Study of the Author's work, "The Sonata: Its Form and Meaning as Exemplified in the Piano Sonatas by Mozart." Paper covers, 2/6.

PURCELL. By WILLIAM H. CUMMINGS, *Mus.Doc.* (Great Musicians Series). Crown 8vo, paper covers, 6/–.

RACHMANINOFF. An Exhilarating Biographical Study of this Genius of the Keyboard. By WATSON LYLE. Preface by LEFF POUISHNOFF. Two Portraits and List of Works. Crown 8vo, cloth, 18/–.

FRANZ SCHUBERT, Man and Composer. A Vivid Story of a Charming Personality. By C. WHITAKER-WILSON. With Original Translations into English of eight Well-known Schubert Songs, together with the Music for the Voice. Portraits and Illustrations of Schubert and his Friends. Crown 8vo, cloth, 15/–.

HENRY SMART'S ORGAN COMPOSITIONS ANALYSED. By J. BROADHOUSE. Crown 8vo, cloth, 5/–.

TEMPLETON AND MALIBRAN. Reminiscences of these Renowned Singers, with Original Letters and Anecdotes. Three Authentic Portraits by MAYALL. 8vo, cloth, 10/–.

WAGNER'S TEACHINGS BY ANALOGY. His Views on Absolute Music and of the Relations of Articulate and Tonal Speech, with Special Reference to "Opera and Drama." By EDWIN EVANS. Crown 8vo, cloth, 6/–; paper, 3/6.

WAGNER'S PARSIFAL. And the Bayreuth Fest-Spielhaus. By N. KILBURN. Paper, 1/–.

WAGNER, 1849. A Historical Retrospect in vindication of Wagner. By WILLIAM ASHTON ELLIS. Cloth, 3/6; paper, 2/–.

OPERA AND DRAMA. By RICHARD WAGNER. Translated by EDWIN EVANS. Opera and the Essence of Music, The Stage-Play and Dramatical Poetic Art in the Abstract, Poetry and Music in the Drama of the Future. 2 vols. Crown 8vo, cloth, 35/–.

The value of the study of Wagner's prose writing as an education to the musical student cannot be over-estimated, and amongst these prose writings "Opera and Drama" may be considered his principal critical and theoretical production. Without a study of its contents no true and lasting understanding of opera can be arrived at.

Wagner writing to his friend Uhlig said:

"*Here you have my testament; I may as well die now—anything further that I could do seems to me a useless piece of luxury.*"

ERNEST NEWMAN in "A Study of Wagner," writes: "Although there appears here and there in his prose-work something of the vast synthetic power of his musical imagination—such a work as 'Opera and Drama,' for instance, finally compelling our admiration for its tenacity of purpose and the breadth of vision that sweeps so far before and after."

WAGNER'S PROSE WORKS. Translated by WM. ASHTON ELLIS. Vol. I, The Art-Work of the Future, etc., 21/–; Vol. II, Opera and Drama, out of print; Vol. III, The Theatre, 21/–; Vol. IV, Art and Politics, 21/–; Vol. V, Actors and Singers, out of print; Vol. VI, Religion and Art, out of print; Vol. VII, In Paris and Dresden, out of print; Vol. VIII, Posthumous, etc., out of print.

HOW TO UNDERSTAND WAGNER'S "RING OF THE NIBELUNG." Being the Story and a Descriptive Analysis of the "Rheingold," the "Valkyr," "Siegfried" and the "Dusk of the Gods." With Musical Examples of the Leading Motives of Each Drama. By GUSTAVE KOBBE. Together with a Sketch of Wagner's Life. By N. KILBURN, *Mus.Bac. Cantab.* Seventh Edition. Crown 8vo, cloth, 10/–.

Description and analysis go hand in hand with the narration of the story. Musical examples are given as aids to the identification of the leading motives and an index makes it easy for any reader to turn up any particular motive instantly.

MY RECOLLECTIONS OF RICHARD WAGNER. By AUGUST LESIMPLE. Post 8vo, cloth, 3/6; paper covers, 2/–.

WAGNER. A sketch of his Life and Works. By N. KILBURN, *Mus.Bac. Cantab.* Paper, 1/–.

ON CONDUCTING. By RICHARD WAGNER. Translated by EDWARD DANNREUTHER. A Treatise on Style in the Execution of Classical Music. Fourth Edition. Crown 8vo, cloth, 8/6.

"One of the finest of his minor publications, and to the professional musician, perhaps the most instructive, giving his views as to the true way of rendering classical music, with numerous directions how to do it, and how not to do it, together with many examples in musical type from the instrumental works of Beethoven, Weber, Mozart, etc."—*Grove's Dictionary.*

WAGNER'S Ring des Nibelungen. The Story of Wagner's "Ring" for English Readers. By N. KILBURN, *Mus.Bac., Cantab.* Crown 8vo, paper, 2/–.

THREE IMPRESSIONS OF BAYREUTH. The 1908 and Previous Wagner Festivals. By ROSE KOENIG. A Record in the Form of a Diary of Visits extending over eight years. Crown 8vo, cloth, 3/6; paper, 2/–.

OUT-OF-PRINT BOOKS.

Positive Microfiches can be supplied of the following books where the printed editions are out of date. They must be used in conjunction with a reader (usually found in large libraries).

ELIZABETHAN VIRGINAL MUSIC AND ITS COMPOSERS. By M. H. GLYN. Second edition, 1934, 20/–.

HISTORY OF THE VIOLONCELLO, Viola da Gamba, etc., with Biographies of all the Most Eminent Players, 1915. By E. VAN DER STRAETEN, 50/–.

HISTORY OF MUSIC AND MUSICAL INSTRUMENTS

STRINGED INSTRUMENTS OF THE MIDDLE AGES. Their Evolution and Development. By HORTENSE PANUM. English edition, revised and edited by JEFFREY PULVER. A detailed and comprehensive history, with illustrations, of the evolution of the mediæval stringed musical instruments from their first appearance in the records of the earliest civilisations, through their gradual development in the Greek, Roman and Christian eras down to more recent times. 400 illustrations. 8vo, cloth, pp. ix, 511, 50/–.

Many years of travel and research were necessary to make the production of this work possible. The author, in addition, has most painstakingly searched mediæval literature and the records of contemporary art for references to and descriptions of the instruments dealt with, and it is believed that the account here given of them is as complete as it is possible to make it.

The book is most generously illustrated and carefully indexed by the editor. No pains have been spared to secure drawings or photographs of practically every type mentioned.

TRIBAL MUSIC AND DANCING IN THE SOUTHERN SUDAN, at Social and Ceremonial Gatherings. A descriptive account of the music, rhythm, etc., from personal observation. By Dr. A. N. TUCKER. 5 illustrations, 61 music examples illustrating the dances, songs and rhythm. 57 pages, demy 8vo, cloth, 10/6.

THE BOWED HARP. A Study of the History of Early Musical Instruments. By OTTO ANDERSSON, *Ph.D.*, *President of the Swedish University at Abo.* From the Original Swedish Edition, revised by the Author. The Translation Edited with additional footnotes by KATHLEEN SCHLESINGER. 116 Illustrations, Bibliography and Index. 340 pages, 8vo, cloth, 30/–.

"A valuable contribution to the literature about early musical instruments."—*The Strad.*

HISTORY OF THE TRUMPET OF BACH AND HANDEL. By WERNER MENKE. Translated by GERALD ABRAHAM. 5 Plates and a Supplement of Music. Crown 8vo, cloth, 18/–.

This history of the trumpet from its earliest use as an artistic instrument, gives special reference to its employment by Bach and Handel. The correct modern performance of the old parts is discussed, and a description of a new instrument invented by the author for this purpose is included.

MAKERS OF THE HARPSICHORD AND CLAVICHORD 1440–1840. By DONALD BOALCH, M.A. 32 Plates, 208 pp., 4to, cloth, 84/–.

This work records 820 makers of the harpsichord, spinet, virginal and clavichord from the fifteenth to the nineteenth centuries. It also gives an account of more than 1,000 surviving instruments from their hands, treating of their date, their registers, compass and decoration, their history (traced sometimes right back to the workshop), and their present ownership.

MUSIC OF THE MOST ANCIENT NATIONS, Particularly of the Assyrians, Egyptians and Hebrews; with special reference to Discoveries in Western Asia and in Egypt. By CARL ENGEL, 1864 (reprinted 1929). About 100 illustrations and many music examples. Demy 8vo, cloth, 30/–.

STORY OF INDIAN MUSIC AND ITS INSTRUMENTS. A Study of the Present and a Record of the Past. Together with Sir William Jones' celebrated Treatise on the Musical Modes of the Hindus. With 19 Plates, chiefly of Instruments, 7 Music Illustrations and a Map. By ETHEL ROSENTHAL, *A.R.C.M.*, *F.R.G.S.* Crown 8vo, cloth, 21/–.

THE TROUBADOUR AS MUSICIAN, Past and Present. By C. A. HARRIS. Cloth, 5/–; paper, 2/6.

OPERA STORIES OF TO-DAY AND YESTERDAY, Retold Act by Act (including Wagner's "The Ring" Operas). By EDMONDSTOUNE DUNCAN. Crown 8vo, cloth, 6/6.

A racy account of the plots and histories of fifty famous operas, from Purcell, Gluck and Mozart, to Richard Strauss and Ethel Smyth.

THE SOURCES OF KEYBOARD MUSIC IN ENGLAND. By CHARLES VAN DEN BORREN, translated by J. E. Matthew. 378 pages, 237 music examples. Crown 8vo, cloth, 21/–.

A standard European work of musical scholarship and one which is of vital interest to all students of keyboard music of the 16th and early 17th centuries.

The collection of keyboard music which naturally provides the basis for this study is the Fitzwilliam Virginal Book, and detailed treatment, copiously illustrated with music examples, is given to the various figures—melodic, rhythmic, and harmonic—in this music and to the forms and styles cultivated by composers for the Virginal. Originally published in England in 1915, this book remains the only thorough study of its type, illuminating a most important branch of English and European music.

HISTORY OF RUSSIAN MUSIC. By M. MONTAGU-NATHAN. The Rise and Progress of the Russian School of Composers. With a Survey of their Lives and a Description of their Works. Frontispiece. 2nd Edition, Revised. Crown 8vo, cloth, 15/–.

Mr. Montagu-Nathan's book breaks new ground; it introduces the English reader to a number of composers, many of whom until recently were nothing more than names.

INTRODUCTORY SKETCH OF IRISH MUSICAL HISTORY. By W. H. GRATTAN FLOOD. A compact Record of the Progress of Music in Ireland during 1,000 Years. Portraits. Crown 8vo, cloth, 5/6; paper, 3/–.

RISE AND DEVELOPMENT OF OPERA. Embracing a Comparative View of the Art in Italy, Germany, France and England. By JOSEPH GODDARD. Showing the Cause of the Falling Back of the English School in the Modern Period, and the Compensation which that Involved. Numerous Music Examples, Portraits and Facsimiles. Crown 8vo, cloth, 12/6.

RISE AND DEVELOPMENT OF MILITARY MUSIC. By Dr. H. G. FARMER. With Illustrations of Early Instruments and Music Examples, and Short Biographical Notices of all the Staff Bandmasters. Crown 8vo, cloth, 15/–.

CATECHISM OF MUSICAL HISTORY AND BIOGRAPHY. With Especial Reference to the English School. By F. J. CROWEST. 187 pages. Post 8vo, cloth, 5/–; paper, 2/6.

POLISH MUSIC AND CHOPIN, ITS LAUREATE. A Historical Account from 995 to the Present Time, including Chopin and his Works. By E. Rayson. Four Portraits. Square 8vo, cloth, 5/–; paper, 3/6.

NATIONAL MUSIC OF THE WORLD. By H. F. Chorley. Edited by H. G. Hewlett. Many Music Examples. Third Edition. Crown 8vo, cloth, 10/6.

Treats of the national tunes, folk-songs and airs of various races of the world. The chapters are undoubtedly marked in a high degree with the critic's acumen, attesting the wide range of Chorley's learning.

CHRONOMETRICAL CHART OF MUSICAL HISTORY. Presenting a Bird's Eye View from the Pre-Christian Era to the XXth Century. By C. A. Harris, *A.R.C.O.*, etc. On linen, 5/–; on paper, 2/6.

HISTORICAL FACTS FOR THE ARABIAN MUSICAL INFLUENCE ON MUSICAL THEORY. By Henry George Farmer, *M.A.*, *Ph.D.* Crown 8vo, cloth, 35/–.

Dr. Farmer's researches into the Music of the Arabs of the Middle Ages, a period when these people led the world's culture, have universal recognition. He now throws a flood of fresh light on many obscure corners in the History of Mediæval Music.

The present work undoubtedly breaks fresh ground in history, and is from the hands of a scholar.

THE PAST AND THE FUTURE. An Inaugural Lecture at Gresham College, 1890. By Sir F. Bridge, *Mus.Doc.* Crown 8vo, 1/–.

THE WORLD'S EARLIEST MUSIC. Traced to its Beginnings in Ancient Lands. By collected Evidences of Relics, Records, History and Musical Instruments, from Greece, Etruria, Egypt, China, through Assyria and Babylonia to the Primitive Home, the Land of Akkad and Sumer. By Hermann Smith. With sixty-five Illustrations, nearly 400 pages. Crown 8vo, cloth, 21/–.

TREATISE ON BYZANTINE MUSIC. By S. G. Hatherley. 208 Music Examples. 162 pages, 4to, cloth, 25/–.

There are upwards of 50 unabbreviated musical pieces, ancient and modern, from Greek, Russian, Turkish and Egyptian sources, given and fully analysed.

OLD ENGLISH PSALMODY. By W. T. Brooke. First Series: From the Accession of Edward VI to the Restoration of Charles II, 1547–1660. Second Series: Psalmists from 1660–1800. Third Series: unpublished. Crown 8vo, paper covers, 3/6 each series.

THE GIPSY IN MUSIC. By Franz Liszt. Translated by Edwin Evans.

Gipsy and Jew, Two Wandering Races.
Gipsy Life in Relation to Art.
Gipsy Music and Musicians.

The result of the Author's long Experience and Investigations of the Gipsies and their Music. With Portraits of the Author etc. Two volumes, demy 8vo, cloth, 30/–.

CHAMBER MUSIC AND ITS MASTERS IN THE PAST AND IN THE PRESENT. By Dr. N. Kilburn. New Edition, revised, and with additional chapters by Gerald Abraham. With Plates and Music Illustrations. Crown 8vo, cloth, 18/–.

The opportunity of the issue of a new edition of the late Dr. Kilburn's book has been taken to bring it thoroughly up-to-date by necessary alterations and additional chapters. Notes have also been inserted on one or two older composers who have not previously been included. The principal additions are the concluding part of Chapter II, part of the survey of Beethoven's chamber music (the quartets in particular), the sections on Smetana, Grieg, Franck and Wolf, almost the whole of Chapter IX, and Chapters X and XI in entirety.

The book now gives us a discussion on the most important writers and projectors of chamber music, from the days of the Stuarts onwards through the period of Frederick the Great up to the present century.

HISTORY OF THE HARP. From the Earliest Period. By John Thomas (*Pencerdd Gwalia*). 8vo, paper covers, 6/–.

THE STORY OF MINSTRELSY. By EDMONDSTOUNE DUNCAN. The whole body of Secular Music that has stood the test of time and which can be called national. Early Gleemen, the Minstrels (church and social), Troubadours, the Tudor period, the great Elizabethanists, etc. Pp. xvi, 337, 18/–.

THE STORY OF MUSICAL FORM. By C. LUCAS. The General Principles of the Art of Composition and how they have been arrived at; explaining the development of the scale, of tonic and dominant, cadences, phrases and motives, counterpoint, canon and fugue, harmony, style, song form, variations, sonata form. Pp. xvi, 226, 18/–.

ORCHESTRAL

ORCHESTRAL AND BAND INSTRUMENTS. A Short Account of the Instruments used in the Orchestra, and in Brass and Military Bands. By G. F. BROADHEAD, *Mus.B. Dunelm, L.Mus.T.C.L.* With 24 Illustrative Music Examples. Post 8vo, cloth, 5/–.

METHOD OF INSTRUMENTATION. How to Write for the Orchestra and Arrange an Orchestral or Band Score. Illustrated with Music Examples and various large folding Charts and Index. By EDWIN EVANS. Demy 8vo, cloth, two volumes.
Vol. I. How to Write for Strings, Arrangement of Scoring and Preparation of Parts. With Charts. 10/–.
Vol. II. How to Write for Wood, Brass and Drums, and Arrange a Band Score. With large folding Charts. 10/–.

INSTRUMENTS AND ART OF THE ORCHESTRA. An Introductory Study. With Table showing Range of each Instrument. By P. W. DE COURCY-SMALE, *Mus.Bac.* Cloth, 6/–.

ORCHESTRAL WIND INSTRUMENTS, Ancient and Modern Being an Account of the Origin and Evolution of Wind Instruments from the Earliest Times. By U. DAUBENY, 11 plates illustrating 61 Instruments or Parts. 8vo, cloth, 21/–.

HANDBOOK ON THE TECHNIQUE OF CONDUCTING. By SIR ADRIAN BOULT. Seventh Edition, revised. 5/–.

THE CONDUCTOR, THE THEORY OF HIS ART. By HECTOR BERLIOZ. Translated by J. BROADHOUSE. With 41 Diagrams and Examples. Crown 8vo, cloth, 7/6; paper covers, 4/–.

PRACTICAL GUIDE FOR THE CONDUCTOR and Useful Notes for the Orchestra. By F. W. DE MASSI-HARDMAN. With Music Examples and Diagrams. 3/–.

HOW TO PLAY FROM SCORE. Treatise on Accompaniment from Score on the Organ or Piano. By F. FETIS. Translated by A. WHITTINGHAM. With forty pages of Examples. Crown 8vo, cloth, 7/6.

This popular and useful book might have been entitled "The Art of Making Arrangements for the Organ or Pianoforte from Full Orchestral and Other Scores." It contains all that is necessary to know upon this subject.

ON CONDUCTING. By RICHARD WAGNER. Translated by E. DANNREUTHER. Fourth Edition. Crown 8vo, cloth, 8/6.

WEINGARTNER, speaking of this celebrated work, said: "Wagner's book laid the foundation for a new understanding of the function of the conductor, in whom we now recognise, not only the eternal factor that holds together an orchestral, choral or operatic performance, but above all the spiritualising internal factor that gives the performance its very soul."

Grove's Dictionary says: "One of the finest of his minor publications, and to a professional musician perhaps the most instructive. A Treatise on *Style*, giving his views as to the true way of rendering classical music, with minute directions how to do it and how not to do it, together with many examples in musical type from the instrumental works of Beethoven, Weber, Mozart, etc."

NOTES ON CONDUCTORS AND CONDUCTING. By T. R. CROGER, *F.R.G.S.*, *F.Z.S.*, also the Organising and Conducting of Amateur Orchestras, with three full-page Illustrations of the various "Beats" and Plan of the Orchestra. Revised and Enlarged. Crown 8vo, cloth, 6/–; paper, 3/–.

ORGAN

MODERN ORGAN BUILDING. By WALTER & THOMAS LEWIS (Organ Builders). Practical Explanation and Description of Organ Construction with especial regard to Pneumatic Action and Chapters on Tuning, Voicing, etc. Third Edition, Revised. 116 Illustrations, including 76 Drawn to Scale and Reproduced from actual Working Drawings. 4to, cloth, 35/–.

The authors, Walter and Thomas Lewis, themselves organ builders, have produced a book which should prove of great value, not only to those who build organs, but also to those who play them. It is a practical explanation and description of organ construction with especial regard to pneumatic action, and no less than 76 reduced scale diagrams, made from actual working drawings, are included. By enlarging the (reduced) actual working drawings to full size, an amateur organ builder should find very little difficulty in constructing an instrument similar (or with modifications) to the one on Plate 41 (a small two manual). Similar working drawings for a three manual organ are also included.

A vast amount of detail is given concerning bellows, building frames, swell boxes, blowing, etc.; there are a number of valuable tables of measurements (pipe scales, borings, etc.) and a descriptive and detailed list of generally used stops.

There is a considerable section on the tonal side of organ building, including the production of sound, voicing and tuning.

This book will appeal to the professional organist, to his more actively interested hearers, and to the enthusiast who happens to be the possessor of a small organ, as well as to amateur and professional organ builders.

TECHNICS OF THE ORGAN. An Illuminative Treatise on many Points and Difficulties connected therewith. Special Treatment of Rhythm, Minimisation of the Use of Accessories, Extemporisation, Expressive Regulation of Organ Tone and Accompaniment. By EDWIN EVANS, *F.R.C.O.* With over 100 Music Examples. 4to, cloth, 12/6.

A valuable Book to help a Moderate Player to become a Master.

NEW ORGAN PRINCIPLES AND THEIR INTERPRETATION. A Guide to and Suggestions on Phrasing and Registration with a view to improved Organ Playing. By TERENCE WHITE. With 54 music examples. Demy 8vo, paper covers, 3/6.

ORGAN OF THE ANCIENTS FROM EASTERN SOURCES (Hebrew, Syriac and Arabic). By HENRY GEORGE FARMER, *M.A., Ph.D., Carnegie Research Fellow*. Foreword by CANON F. W. GALPIN. With numerous Illustrations. 8vo, cloth, 35/–.

This, his latest work, yet further enhances the world-wide reputation that Dr. Farmer's studies in Arabian music have already won for him. Important details in the history of the organ hitherto unknown are revealed in these translations from Hebrew, Syriac and Arabic treatises.

"An authoritative treatment of the subject."—*Grove's Dictionary*.

TECHNICS OF ORGAN TEACHING. A Handbook which treats of Special Points in Organ Teaching Examinations, together with Test Questions. By R. A. JEVONS. Boards, 3/6.

ART OF ORGAN ACCOMPANIMENT IN THE CHURCH SERVICES. What to Do and what to Avoid: being a Guide to the Organist in the effective rendering of the Music. By WALTER L. TWINNING, *F.R.C.O.* Boards, 3/6.

THE ORGAN AS VIEWED FROM WITHIN. A Practical Handbook on the Mechanism of the Organ. By JOHN BROADHOUSE. With over fifty Illustrations. Crown 8vo, cloth, 15/–.

LECTURE ON THE PEDAL ORGAN. Its History, Design and Control. By THOMAS CASSON. With folding Diagram. 8vo cloth, 6/–.

THE EARLY ENGLISH ORGAN BUILDERS and their Works, from the Fifteenth Century to the Period of the Great Rebellion By DR. E. F. RIMBAULT. Post 8vo, cloth, 7/6.

THE ORGAN, WRITINGS AND OTHER UTTERANCES ON ITS STRUCTURE, HISTORY, PROCURAL, CAPABILITIES, ETC. By F. W. WARMAN. Four Parts (A to Nou, the rest unprinted), royal 8vo, paper covers, 15/–.

The parts advertised above are all that have been published, as the untimely death of Mr. Warman prevented the completion of the work. The book is a mine of information for those keen on organ subjects. The author devoted the best part of his life to compiling the work and collecting material for his subject.

SOME CONTINENTAL ORGANS and their Makers. With Specifications of many of the fine Examples in Germany and Switzerland. By JAMES I. WEDGWOOD. Post 8vo, cloth, 6/6.

Contains specification and a brief *critique* of some of the famous old Continental organs. Amongst others particulars are given of those at Haarlem, Cologne, Aix-la-Chapelle, Frankfort, Heidelberg, Ulm, Stuttgart, Einsiedein, Strassburg and Antwerp. This work forms a valuable supplement to Hopkins's and Rimbault's great treatise.

MODERN ORGAN TUNING, The How and Why, Clearly Explaining the Nature of the Organ Pipe and the System of Equal Temperament, together with an Historic Record of the Evolution of the Diatonic Scale from the Greek Tetrachord. By HERMANN SMITH. Crown 8vo, cloth, 10/6.

THE INFLUENCE OF THE ORGAN IN HISTORY. By DUDLEY BUCK. Crown 8vo, boards, 4/–; paper covers, 2/–.

INTERNATIONAL REPERTOIRE GUIDE (Historical, Educational and Descriptive) to Foreign, British and American Works. By HERBERT WESTERBY. 4to, cloth, 21/–.

Describes the best Organ Music of foreign countries as well as of Britain and America.

A large and beautifully presented quarto work, fully illustrated by thirty-six plates on fine art paper, comprising seven English and sixteen foreign organs, thirty-one portraits, and illustrations of the houses of Bach and Handel.

REFORM IN ORGAN BUILDING. By THOMAS CASSON. Demy 8vo, 2/6.

THE BYRD ORGAN BOOK, for Piano or Organ. A Collection of 21 Pieces (Pavans, Galliards, etc.), by William Byrd, 1543–1623, edited from the Virginal MSS., and now first published in Modern Notation. By M. H. GLYN. 7/6.

ADVICE TO YOUNG ORGANISTS. By J. T. Field. 6d.

THE ORGAN FIFTY YEARS HENCE. A Study of its Development in the Light of its Past History and Present Tendencies. By Francis Burgess, *F.S.A.*, *Scot.*, 1908. Demy 8vo. 2/-.

PIANOFORTE

NATURAL TECHNICS IN PIANO MASTERY. A Complete and authoritative Manual, covering every Phase of Piano Playing and Study—tracing in simple Steps for the Student's Guidance the aesthetic Steps as well as the technical Problems leading from Beginning Stages to Concert Artistry. By JACOB EISENBERG. 55 illustrations. Crown 8vo, cloth, 12/6.

THE APPROACH TO LISZT. A Course of Modern Tonal-Technique for the Piano, in the form of Graded Studies from the Moderately Difficult to the Master Stage. By HERBERT WESTERBY, *Mus.Bac. Lond., F.R.C.O., etc.* Folio, 5/6.

Preliminary Studies in Touch and Phrasing in all Keys. Based on the Scales and Broken Chords.

Intermediate Studies in Sequential, Wrist and Preparatory Arpeggio Work in the Black and White Key Positions.

Advanced Sequential Studies on the Black Keys, with Sixteen Excerpts from Liszt's Piano Works. The Master Works: Fifty-eight Excerpts from Liszt.

THE ART OF TUNING THE PIANOFORTE. A New Comprehensive Treatise to enable the Musician to Tune his Piano upon the System founded on the Theory of Equal Temperament. By HERMANN SMITH. New Edition, Revised. Crown 8vo, limp cloth, 7/6.

EXTEMPORISING AT THE PIANO MADE EASY. A Manual for Beginners in Musical Composition. Hints and Aids for the "From Brain to Keyboard" Composer. By REV. E. H. MELLING, *F.R.C.O.* 8vo, 2/–.

INDIVIDUALITY IN PIANO TOUCH. By ALGERNON H. LINDO and J. ALFRED JOHNSTONE. Crown 8vo, 2/6.

THE ARTIST AT THE PIANO. Essays on the Art of Musical Interpretation. By GEORGE WOODHOUSE. 8vo, cloth, 5/6.

The celebrated pianist, Paderewski, after reading the manuscript of this stimulating volume, wrote: "The booklet is quite a remarkable work and a really valuable contribution to the philosophy of pianistic art."

THE STUDENT'S GUIDE TO THE ART OF TEACHING THE PIANOFORTE. By CYRIL R. H. HORROCKS, *L.R.A.M., L.T.C.L., A.R.C.M.* With an Extensive and Carefully Graded List of Studies and Course of the Great Masters. Numerous Musical Examples. Second edition, Revised. Crown 8vo, cloth, 10/–.

Until quite recently it was thought impossible to give practical instructions on the art of teaching, but the error of this idea has been proved by the great success of the teachers' class at the various musical institutions. The author's aim is to supply a guide-book expressly for beginners and those with limited experience in the art.

PIANOFORTE TEACHER'S GUIDE. By L. PLAIDY. Translated by F. R. RITTER. Crown 8vo, boards, 3/–; paper, 2/–.

CANDIDATE'S SCALE AND ARPEGGIO TESTS for the Piano. In the Primary, Elementary and Junior Grades of all Local Examinations in Music, and the Higher and Lower Divisions of the Associated Board of the R.A.M. and R.C.M. By WILSON MANHIRE. 1/–.

TECHNICAL STUDY IN THE ART OF PIANOFORTE PLAYING (Deppe's Principles). By C. A. EHRENFECHTER. With numerous music examples. Fourth Edition. Crown 8vo, cloth, 6/–.

CONTENTS: Position—Arm—Wrist—Fingers; Touch (Tone Production); Legato; Equality of Tone; Tension and Contraction; Five Finger Exercises; Skips; The Scale; Arpeggio Chords; Firm Chords; High Raising of the Arm; Melody and its Accompaniment; Connection of Firm Chords; The Tremolo; The Shake (Trill); The Pedal; Fingering.

HOW TO ACCOMPANY AT THE PIANO. By EDWIN EVANS. (Plain Accompaniment, Figurated Accompaniment and Practical Harmony for Accompanists.) 172 Music Examples. Crown 8vo, cloth, 7/6.

GRADUATED SCALE AND ARPEGGIO MANUAL. Compiled for the various Exams. By HENRY SAINT-GEORGE. 3/–.

A SYSTEM OF STUDY OF SCALES AND CHORDS. Being Chapters on the Elements of Pianoforte Technique. By B. VINE WESTBROOK, *F.R.C.O.* Numerous Examples. Revised edition. 8vo, 3/–.

The author outlines a scheme which abolishes the drudgery and inspires the pupil with an enthusiasm for practice and formulates a method or system in which that practice may be carried out.

PIANO CLASSES IN ELEMENTARY SCHOOLS. By AUDREY KING. With Music Examples. Crown 8vo, 1/–.

HOW TO PLAY 110 FAVOURITE PIANO SOLOS. Being the 4 Series complete in 1 vol. of "Well-Known Piano Solos: How to Play them with Understanding, Expression and Effect." By CHARLES W. WILKINSON. Crown 8vo, cloth, 12/6.

WELL-KNOWN PIANO SOLOS. How to Play them with Understanding, Expression and Effect. By C. W. WILKINSON. Four Series, 2/– each (each series containing about 26 articles), or four in one vol. as above.

Contents of the First Series:—SINDING, Rustle of Spring. SCARLATTI, Pastorale le Capriccio. PADEREWSKI, Minuet in G. HANDEL, Harmonious Blacksmith. RUBENSTEIN, Melody in F. SCHARWENKA, Polish Dance. SCHUMANN, Nachtstücke. GODARD, Mazurka. DELIBES, Pizzicati from Sylvia. GRIEG, Wedding Day at Troldhangen. ELGAR, Salut d'Amour. PADEREWSKI, Melodie. RAFF, La Fileuse. TCHAIKOVSKY, Troika. GODARD, Berger et Bergères. CHAMINADE, Pierrette. MOSZKOWSKI, Etincelles. PADEREWSKI, Minuet in A major. GRIEG, Norwegian Bridal Procession. LISZT, Regata Veneziana. CHAMINADE, Automne. MOSKOWSKI, Serenata. LACK, Valse Arabesque. SCHUMANN, Arabeske. CHOPIN, Etude in G flat. DURAND, First Valse.

Draws one's attention to the beauties in a piece, explains difficulties here and there, draws attention to a pedal effect and any peculiarity of fingering, and generally gives all the information a professor is expected to give to his pupils.

DELIVERY IN THE ART OF PIANOFORTE PLAYING, On Rhythm, Measure, Phrasing, Tempo. By C. A. EHRENFECHTER. Crown 8vo, cloth, 6/–.

TOUCH, PHRASING AND INTERPRETATION. By J. ALFRED JOHNSTONE. Crown 8vo, cloth, 6/–.

REEVES' VAMPING TUTOR. Art of Extemporaneous Accompaniment, or Playing by Ear on the Pianoforte, Rapidly Enabling anyone having an Ear for Music (with or without any Knowledge of Musical Notation) to Accompany with Equal Facility in any Key. Practical Examples. By FRANCIS TAYLOR. Folio, 2/–.

THE DEPPE FINGER EXERCISES for Rapidly Developing an Artistic Touch in Pianoforte Playing, Carefully Arranged, Classified and Explained by AMY FAY (Pupil of Tausig, Kullak, Liszt and Deppe). Folio, English or Continental Fingering, 2/–.

INTRODUCTION TO RUSSIAN PIANO MUSIC. By HERBERT WESTERBY, *Mus.Bac.Lond.*, *F.R.C.O.*, *L.Mus.T.C.L.*, 1/–.

REEVES' POPULAR PIANOFORTE TUTOR. Rudiments of Music, Exercises with Popular Airs, Major and Minor Scales. With Illustration of Fingerboard. Folio, 2/6.

TECHNICAL AND THEORETICAL

ESSENTIALS IN MUSIC STUDY FOR EXAMINATIONS. A Helpful Guide both for the General Student and Candidates for Junior and Intermediate Examinations. By REV. E. H. MELLING, *F.R.C.O.* Cloth, 5/–; paper covers, 2/6.

Rev. E. H. Melling is the author of several popular works which have been found of great use to music students—"Guide for the Young Composer," "Extemporising at the Piano made Easy," etc.

GUIDE FOR THE YOUNG COMPOSER. Hints on the Art of Composition, with Examples of Easy Application. By REV. E. H. MELLING, *F.R.C.O.* Cloth, 5/–; paper covers, 2/6.

EXAMINATION TEST QUESTIONS. Containing spaces for the Pupils' Written Answers. By WALTER L. TWINNING, *F.R.C.O.* No. 1, Musical Notation and Time; No. 2, Formation of Scales; No. 3, Ornaments; No. 4, Intervals, 9d. each.

THEORY OF MUSIC FOR YOUNG MUSICIANS. With Answers given to all the Questions, and a Dictionary of necessary Musical Terms. By MARY SHARP. 1/6.

102 TEST QUESTIONS ON THE GENERAL RUDIMENTS OF MUSIC. In Groups of Six each Lesson, for Written or Oral Use. By WILSON MANHIRE, *L.R.A.M.* 6d.

PRIMARY COURSE IN THE RUDIMENTS OF MUSIC, With Hints on Answering Questions (Written Work) for All Examinations in the Primary, Elementary and Preparatory Grades. By WILSON MANHIRE, *L.R.A.M.*, etc. 2/–.

EXAMINATION CANDIDATE'S GUIDE to Scale and Arpeggio Piano Playing (with Tests). All that is required for the Various Exams. By WILSON MANHIRE, *L.R.A.M.* 3/–.

STUDIES IN MODULATION for Practical and Theoretical Purposes. By PERCY BAKER, *F.R.C.O.*, etc. 3/–.

HANDBOOK OF MUSICAL FORM. For Instrumental Players and Vocalists. By E. VAN DER STRAETEN. With Musical Examples, 205 pages. Crown 8vo, cloth, 6/6; paper, 4/–.

The part of the work on Dance Forms gives a history and description of the Suite or Partita, Allemande, Courante, Sarabande, Gigue, Gavotte, Musette, Bourrée, Branle, Passepied, Rigaudon, Loure, Pavane, Galliard, Tambourin, Cebell, Rondo, Menuet, Polonaise, Mazurka, Bolero, Tarantella, Saltarello, March, Ciaccone and Passacaglia.

HOW TO COMPOSE WITHIN THE LYRIC FORM. By EDWIN EVANS, *F.R.C.O.* Described for the General Reader, Practically Exemplified for the Musician and Reduced to Precept for the Student. With 60 Music Examples. Crown 8vo, cloth, 6/–.

STUDIES IN HISTORICAL FACTS AND MUSICAL FORM. Being a Guide and Note Book for a more Systematic Preparation of the General Knowledge Papers now set at the Universities and Colleges of Music. By PERCY BAKER. Cloth, 5/6; paper, 3/–.

MUSICAL EXPRESSIONS, PHRASES AND SENTENCES, with their Corresponding Equivalents in French, German and Italian. By F. BERGER. 8vo, cloth, 5/6; paper, 3/–.

RUDIMENTS OF MUSIC, Set forth in Graded QUESTIONS with ANSWERS, for Use of Candidates preparing for the Examinations of R.A.M., R.C.M. and T.C.L. By B. HOWARTH, *L.R.A.M.* and *A.R.C.M.* Crown 8vo, 2/–.

The Answers are always on the right hand page and can be covered over if desired, the Questions being on the corresponding left hand pages.

STEPS IN HARMONY. With Copious Explanatory Examples and Graded Test Exercises. A Handbook for Students. By DR. CHURCHILL SIBLEY. With Music Examples throughout. Crown 8vo, boards, 6/–.

It is believed that he who thoroughly masters the contents of these pages will be prepared to study intelligently the harmonic structure of the works of the great masters, and also to follow critically the changeful tendencies of the present day.

600 QUESTIONS AND 600 EXERCISES IN ELEMENTARY MUSICAL THEORY. By W. H. PALMER. Crown 8vo, 3/–.

Intended as a help to the private student and to the candidate preparing for the several musical examinations.

THE MODAL ACCOMPANIMENT OF PLAIN CHANT. A Practical Treatise. By EDWIN EVANS, Senior, *F.R.C.O.* Part I, Theoretical; Part II, Practical School of Plain Chant Accompaniment, consisting of 240 Exercises, with an Appendix of Notes. Crown 8vo, cloth, 10/–.

THE HARMONISING OF MELODIES. A Textbook for Students and Beginners. By H. C. BANISTER. Third Edition, with numerous Music Examples. Crown 8vo, limp cloth, 5/–.

MUSICAL ANALYSIS. A Handbook for Students. By H. C. BANISTER. With Music Examples. Crown 8vo, limp cloth, 5/–; paper covers, 2/6.

THE ART OF MODULATING. A Series of Papers on Modulating at the Pianoforte. By HENRY C. BANISTER. With 62 Music Examples. Crown 8vo, cloth, 6/–; paper covers, 3/6.

MODERN CHORDS EXPLAINED. (The Tonal Scale in Harmony.) By ARTHUR G. POTTER. Music Examples from Debussy, Strauss and Bantock. 8vo, cloth, 4/–; paper covers, 2/–.

EXERCISES IN FIGURED BASS AND MELODY HARMONIZATION. By JAMES LYON, *Mus.Doc.* 4to, 3/6.

EXAMPLES OF FOUR-PART WRITING FROM FIGURED BASSES AND GIVEN MELODIES. By JAMES LYON, *Mus.Doc.* 4to, 5/6.

These exercises are printed in open score so as to be of use in score reading tests. This volume forms a key to "Exercises in Figured Bass" by the same author (see above).

THE RUDIMENTS OF GREGORIAN MUSIC. By FRANCIS BURGESS, *F.S.A., Scot.* Crown 8vo, limp cloth, 2/6; paper, 1/6.

MUSICAL PRONOUNCING DICTIONARY. By DR. DUDLEY BUCK. Eighth Edition, with the Concise Explanation and Pronunciation of each Term. Edited and Revised by A. WHITTINGHAM. Crown 8vo, 1/6.

A most valuable and useful little book to all musical people. The method adopted for giving the pronunciation of each term is most concise and clear.

HARMONY, EASILY AND PROGRESSIVELY ARRANGED. Presenting in a Simple Manner the Elementary Ideas as well as the Introduction to the Study of Harmony. With about 300 Music Examples and Exercises. By PAUL COLBERG. Crown 8vo, cloth 7/6; paper covers, 3/6.

COMPEND OF MUSICAL KNOWLEDGE. By PERCY BAKER, *F.R.C.O., L.Mus.T.C.L.* Being a Guide with Notes, Hints and Articles on the Study of Examination Questions. Crown 8vo, cloth, 6/–; paper, 3/6.

Primarily to help candidates entering for the R.C.O. and T.C.L. Diplomas, though containing much information for the amateur musician and general reader. Indispensable to teachers in guiding their pupils through a course of study dealing with a large number of subjects like those set for the F.R.C.O. and A.R.C.O.

ELEMENTARY MUSIC. A Book for Beginners. By DR. WESTBROOK. With Questions and Vocal Exercises. Crown 8vo, cloth, 4/–; paper, 2/–.

CONTENTS: 1. The Staff and its Clefs. 2. Notes and their Rests. 3. Bars and Time. 4. Accidentals. 5. Keys and Scales. 6. Intervals. 7. Musical Pitch. 8. Accent. 9. Secondary Signs. 10. Ornaments and Groups of Notes. 11. Voices and Scores. 12. Church Modes. 13. Italian and other Directions. 14. Foreign Note-Names. 15. Questions. 16. Vocal Exercises.

"His explanations are extremely clear. The questions at the end will be found very useful."—*Musical Times.*

EXERCISES ON GENERAL ELEMENTARY MUSIC. A Book for Beginners. By K. PAIGE. Part I, 1/6; Part II, 2/–.

CONTENTS OF PART I: 1. Pitch. 2. Length of Sounds. 3. Time. 4. Time and Accent. 5. Intervals. 6. Scales. 7. Transposition. 8. Syncopation. 9. Signs and Abbreviations. 10. Notation. 11. Miscellaneous Questions and Exercises.

CONTENTS OF PART II: 1. Triads. 2. First Inversion of a Triad. 3. Second Inversion of a Triad. 4. Dissonances. 5. Suspensions. 6. Sequences. 7. Cadences. 8. Dominant Sevenths, etc.

HOW TO MEMORISE MUSIC. By C. F. KENYON. With numerous Music Examples. Crown 8vo, cloth, 6/–.

HOW TO HARMONIZE MELODIES. With Hints on Writing for Strings and Pianoforte Accompaniments. By J. HENRY BRIDGER, *Mus.Bac.* With Music Examples. Crown 8vo, cloth, 6/–.

THE ART OF MODULATION. A Handbook showing at a Glance the Modulations from one Key to any other in the Octave, consisting of 1,008 Modulations. For the Use of Organists and Musical Directors. Edited by CARLI ZOELLER. 4to, paper covers, 5/–.

THE STUDENT'S BOOK OF CHORDS. With an Explanation of their Inversions and Resolutions. By PASCAL NEEDHAM. Crown 8vo, 1/6.

The chords with their inversions and resolutions are briefly and clearly explained.

TRANSPOSITION AT SIGHT. For Students of the Organ and Pianoforte. By H. E. NICHOL. Fourth Edition, with numerous Musical Exercises. Crown 8vo, 2/-.

The practice of transposing upon the lines here laid down develops the "mental ear," quickens the musical perception and gives ease in sight reading; as it is evident that, if the student can *transpose* at sight, he will not have much difficulty in merely *playing* at sight. Free use is made of the tonic sol-fa as well as the standard notation in many musical examples.

SCHUMANN'S RULES AND MAXIMS FOR YOUNG MUSICIANS. Sewed, 6d.

MUSICAL ACOUSTICS. (Student's Helmholtz), or the Phenomena of Sound as Connected with Music. By JOHN BROADHOUSE. With more than 100 Illustrations. Fifth Impression. Crown 8vo, cloth, 15/-.

"In his Preface the author says: 'The object of the present book is to give, in one volume, a good general view of the subject to those who can neither spare time to read, nor money to buy a number of large and expensive works.' A perusal of the book justifies us in asserting that this design is most satisfactorily carried out; and it is not too much to say that although the plan of the work excludes the possibility of minutely dissecting every subject treated upon, any careful reader may obtain so clear an insight into the principle of acoustics, as to enable him not only to pass an examination but to store up a large amount of general knowledge upon the phenomena of sound."—*Musical Times.*

VIOLIN AND STRINGED INSTRUMENTS

GERMAN VIOLIN MAKERS. By FRIDOLIN HAMMA. A Critical Dictionary of German Violin Makers with a Series of Plates Illustrating Characteristic and Fine Examples of their Work. Translated by Walter Stewart. 64 pages of text and 80 plates in half-tone, 12 × 10 inches, cloth, 105/–.

This book is written by one of the most prominent experts in Europe, this status assuring the importance of his contribution to violin connoisseurship.

About 80 fine German instruments are represented in the plates of this book, the majority by two views, whilst many are extra-illustrated by separate scroll pictures. Good, representative examples of the German masters were selected for the purpose of providing the most informative illustrations, and a short descriptive general treatment accompanies each maker's name in the text. The arrangement of the text is on an alphabetical plan.

Fridolin Hamma's book is one of the most important contributions of our time to violin literature, a work which no connoisseur or maker should miss.

VIOLIN TECHNICS, or How to Become a Violinist. Exact Instructions, Step by Step, for its Accomplishment with or without a Teacher. By "FIRST VIOLIN." 3/–.

PLAYING AT SIGHT FOR VIOLINISTS and Others in an Orchestra. Valuable Hints and Aids for its Mastery. By SYDNEY TWINN. Post 8vo, 3/–.

TONAL SCALES AND ARPEGGIOS FOR VIOLIN. Introductory to the Unusual Intonation and Finger-grouping of Advanced Modern Music. By SYDNEY TWINN. Folio, 3/–.

"These scales will be useful to advanced players who find difficulties in the unusual intonation and technique of modern music."—*Strad.*

ARPEGGIOS FOR THE VIOLIN. By Basil Althaus. Folio. 3/–.

VIOLINIST'S ENCYCLOPÆDIC DICTIONARY. Containing the Explanation of about 4,000 Words, Phrases, Signs, References, etc., Foreign, as well as English, used in the Study of the Violin, and also by String Players generally, by F. B. Emery, *M.A.* New and enlarged edition. 246 pp., crown 8vo. Cloth, 12/6; or printed on India paper, suitable for student or travel, 15/–.

70 PREPARATORY VIOLIN EXERCISES for Beginners in the First Position, carefully Graduated, Supplementary to the First Instruction Book. By Wilson Manhire, *L.R.A.M., A.R.C.M., etc.* 2/6.

BOW INSTRUMENTS, their Form and Construction. Practical and Detailed Investigation and Experiments regarding Vibration, Sound Results, and Construction. By J. W. Giltay. Numerous Diagrams. 8vo, cloth, 16/–.

"A valuable treatise."—*The Strad.*

OLD VIOLINS AND VIOLIN LORE, Famous Makers of Cremona and Brescia, and of England, France and Germany (with Biographical Dictionary), Famous Players, and Chapters on Varnish, Strings and Bows, with 13 full-page plates. By H. R. Haweis. Demy 8vo, cloth, 25/–.

A delightful informal account of famous makers, players and collectors. In matters pertaining to old violins, the author is known as a specialist and, moreover, one who writes in a pleasant flowing style, which cannot be said of all specialists. He discourses about Italian, French and English violins, about varnish, strings, bows, violin dealers, collectors and amateurs. There are some fine plates, a dictionary of violin makers and a bibliography. This book is one for reading, and also for reference, and in its lighter pages for recreation.

YOUNG VIOLINIST'S SCALE AND ARPEGGIO MANUAL. By Wilson Manhire, *L.R.A.M., etc.* 2/–.

NOTABLE VIOLIN SOLOS: How to Play Them. Three Series (consisting of 44 descriptive Articles in all). By E. VAN DER STRAETEN. 2/6 each series. Also complete in boards, with Portraits, 10/–.

VIOLIN MANUFACTURE IN ITALY and its German Origin. By DR. E. SCHEBEK. Translated by W. E. LAWSON. Second Edition. Square 12 mo, cloth, 6/–; paper, 3/6.

CHATS WITH VIOLINISTS. By WALLACE RITCHIE. Crown 8vo, cloth, 8/6.

CHAPTERS: On the Importance of being Accurate; On Various Details; On the Violin and its Fittings; On Reading from Sight and Playing from Memory; A Few Violin Secrets; Some Valuable Technical Exercises; Hand Development for Violinists, including Eighteen Excellent Finger Gymnastics; Sundry Useful Hints.

I here lay before the public that information and advice which I have hitherto been content to reserve for the sole use of my own pupils. During a considerable experience, both as a student and as a teacher of the violin, I have naturally pieced together quite a variety of small hints and items of information which, though modest enough individually, have been found on the whole to be of no inconsiderable value, not only with regard to my own playing, but also—and which is of far more importance—in enabling me to impart a knowledge of the art to others.

ADVICE TO VIOLIN STUDENTS. Containing Information of the Utmost Value to every Violinist. By WALLACE RITCHIE. Crown 8vo, cloth, 7/6; paper, 5/–.

CONTENTS: Selecting and Adjusting—Choice of a Teacher—Course of Study—The Sevcik Method—Practising—Style—Tone Production—Pronunciation of Terms, Names, etc.—Graded List of Studies, Pieces, etc. Together with Hints on Common Faults—Shifting — Reading Music — Stopping — Harmonics — Vibrato —Tempo—Intonation, Pitch, etc.

INFORMATION FOR PLAYERS, Owners, Dealers and Makers of Bow Instruments, also for String Manufacturers. Taken from Personal Experiences, Studies and Observations. By WILLIAM HEPWORTH. Crown 8vo, cloth, 8/6.

CONTENTS: The Pegs—Neck—Finger-board—Bridge—Tail-piece—Saddle—Violin Holder—Tail-pin—Bar—Sound-post—On the Stringing of Bow Instruments in General Use—Strings—Rosin—Cleaning of the Instrument and the Bridge—Bow—Violin Case—Repairs—Preservation—Conclusion.

SKETCHES OF GREAT PIANISTS AND GREAT VIOLINISTS. Biographical and Anecdotal, with Account of the Violin and Early Violinists. Viotti, Spohr, Paganini, De Beriot, Ole Bull, Clementi, Moscheles, Schumann (Robert and Clara), Chopin, Thalberg, Gottschalk, Liszt. By G. T. FERRIS. Third Edition. Crown 8vo, cloth, 8/6.

TREATISE ON THE STRUCTURE AND PRESERVATION OF THE VIOLIN and all other Bow Instruments. By JACOB AUGUSTUS OTTO. Together with an Account of the most Celebrated Makers and of the Genuine Characteristics of their Instruments. Translated by JOHN BISHOP. Fourth Edition. Crown 8vo, cloth, 12/6.

The author of this book on the structure of the violin was at one time the violin maker to the Court of the Grand Duke of Weimar. In addition to over thirty years practical experience in the repairing of stringed instruments, he had a sound theoretical knowledge of music, as well as mathematics, physics and acoustics.

He gives detailed information on the construction of the violin and other bow instruments, with notes on how to distinguish between genuine Italian instruments and spurious imitations.

The book also includes sections on the care of instruments, strings, bows, rosin, etc. A method of tracing a model for a violin is described.

HOW TO PLAY THE FIDDLE. For Beginners on the Violin. By H. W. and G. GRESSWELL. Eighth Edition. Crown 8vo, 2 parts, paper covers, 1/6 each.

BIOGRAPHICAL DICTIONARY OF FIDDLERS. Including Performers on the Violoncello and Double Bass. By A. MASON CLARKE. 9 Portraits. Post 8vo, cloth, 10/-.

ART OF HOLDING THE VIOLIN AND BOW AS EXEMPLIFIED BY OLE BULL. His Pose and Method proved to be based on true Anatomical Principles. By A. B. CROSBY, *M.D., Professor of Anatomy*. Portrait, Diagrams and Illustrations. 8vo, cloth, 6/–.

Included in the above are some interesting recollections and anecdotes of Ole Bull.

THE VIOLIN AND OLD VIOLIN MAKERS. Being a Historical and Biographical Account of the Violin. By A. MASON CLARKE. With Facsimile of Labels used by Old Masters. Crown 8vo, cloth, 10/–.

THE VIOLIN, ITS HISTORY AND CONSTRUCTION. Illustrated and Described from many Sources. Together with a List of Italian and Tyrolese Makers. With 28 Illustrations and folding Examples of the First Music issued for the Lute, Fiddle and Voice. By ABELE and NIEDERHEITMANN. Translated by J. BROADHOUSE. Crown 8vo, cloth, 12/6.

The learned and instructive treatise of Abele, skilfully rendered by J. Broadhouse and supplemented by a version of Niederheitmann's list of Italian and Tyrolese violin makers.

HOW TO MAKE A VIOLIN. By J. BROADHOUSE. Revised Edition. Folding Plates and many Diagrams, Figures, etc. Crown 8vo, cloth, 10/6.

CONTENTS: Introduction—The Parts of the Violin—On the Selection of Wood—The Tools required—The Models—The Mould—The Side-pieces and Side Linings—The Back—Of the Belly—The Thickness of the Back and Belly—The Bass Bar—The Purfling—The Neck—The Finger-board—The Nut and String Guard—Varnishing and Polishing—Varnishes and Colouring Matter—The Varnish—A Mathematical Method of Constructing the Outline—The Remaining Accessories of the Violin.

This new edition had the advantage of being revised throughout by a celebrated violin maker.

A MUSICAL ZOO. Twenty-four Illustrations displaying the Ornamental Application of Animal Forms to Musical Instruments (Violins, Viol da Gambas, Guitars, Pochette, Serpent, etc.). Drawn from the Carved Examples by HENRY SAINT-GEORGE. Cloth, 6/–; paper, 3/6.

THE HISTORY OF THE VIOLIN and other Instruments Played on with the Bow from the Remotest Times to the Present. Also an Account of the Principal Makers. Coloured Frontispiece and numerous Illustrations and Figures. By W. SANDYS, *F.S.A.*, and S. A. FORSTER. Demy 8vo, cloth, 35/–.

This well-known book, first published in 1864, is especially valuable in connection with the instrument makers of the English school, and is the chief literary source of information concerning our old native craftsmen. It is good to bear in mind that as Simon Forster was a skilled and experienced instrument worker, the technical notes to be discovered in the pages of this book in which he collaborated are worthy of attention.

AN IMPORTANT LESSON TO PERFORMERS ON THE VIOLIN. By the Celebrated TARTINI. Portrait. Translated by DR. BURNEY, issued originally in 1779, together with the original Italian. 8vo, boards, 6/–.

VIOLONCELLO EXERCISES, SCALES AND ARPEGGIOS. By E. GILLET. Part I, Exercises, 1/6; Part II, Scales, 1/6 and Part III, Arpeggios, 1/6.

ART OF VIOLONCELLO PLAYING. Tutor in Three Books. By E. VAN DER STRAETEN. Text in English and French. 4to. Book I, 3/6; Book II, 4/–; Book III, unpublished.

WELL-KNOWN VIOLONCELLO SOLOS. How to Play Them. Three Series. By E. VAN DER STRAETEN. 2/6 each series. Also complete in cloth, with Portraits, 10/–.

HOW TO REPAIR VIOLINS and other Musical Instruments. By ALFRED F. COMMON. With Diagrams. Crown 8vo, cloth, 8/6.

ROYSTON'S PROGRESSIVE VIOLIN TUTOR (with Illustrations giving Correct Position for Hand, Wrist and Fingers). Folio, 3/–.

VOCAL

SUCCESS IN AMATEUR OPERA. Instructions on Auditions, Equipment of the Society and the Conductor, Allocation of Rôles, Rehearsals, Training of Soloists, Diction, Conducting, etc. By HUBERT BROWN. Including a Section on Stage Management, by H. G. TOY. Crown 8vo, cloth, 6/–.

SPEECH DISTINCT AND PLEASING, or Why not Learn to Speak Correctly? A clear description of the mental and physical qualities on which the art of good speaking is founded. By FRANK PHILIP. 162 pages, Crown 8vo, cloth, 7/–; paper covers, 4/–.

VOICE PRODUCTION FOR ELOCUTION AND SINGING. By REV. E. H. MELLING. Music Examples. 31 pages, f'cap 8vo, cloth, 4/–; paper covers, 2/–.

TEXTBOOK OF VOCAL TRAINING AND PREPARATION FOR SONG INTERPRETATION. With a Section showing how to Determine Accurately by Pitch and Curve Graphs the special Suitability of Songs selected for particular Vocal Requirements. Music Illustrations and Descriptive Diagrams. By FRANK PHILIP. 8vo, cloth, 15/–.

THE AMATEUR VOCALIST. A Guide to Singing. With Useful Hints on Voice Production, Song Preparation, etc. By WALTER L. TWINNING, *F.R.C.O.* Post 8vo, limp cloth, 2/–.

HOW TO TEACH CLASS SINGING, and a Course of Outline Lessons which illustrate the psychological principles upon which successful tuition is based. By GRANVILLE HUMPHREYS, Professor of the Art of Teaching, Voice Production, etc., at the T.S.-F.C.; late Lecturer in Class Singing at the Training School for Music Teachers. Numerous Music Illustrations. Cloth, 10/–.

Teachers will find this very striking book of great value. The publishers have no hesitation in strongly recommending it.

THE VOICE AND SINGING. Practically Explained, Condensed but Comprehensive Treatise, designed principally for Students and Amateurs, by an Experienced Singer and Teacher (C. W. PALMER). Cloth, 5/–; paper, 2/6.

"I have studied the subject as an enthusiast both theoretically and practically, both as student and teacher, for over thirty years."—*Extract from the Preface.*

VOCAL SUCCESS, or Thinking and Feeling in Speech and Song, including a Chapter on Ideal Breathing for Health. By the REV. CHAS. GIB. Crown 8vo, cloth, 5/–; paper covers, 2/6.

The known facts of science in connection with both the structure and functions of the vocal organs are stated; and have been supplemented by impressions formed in the course of long experience and experiment in the training of voices.

VOCAL SCIENCE AND ART. Hints on Production of Musical Tone. By REV. CHAS. GIB. The Boy's Voice, Muscular Relaxation, Art of Deep Breathing, Elocution for Ordination Candidates. Crown 8vo, cloth, 6/–.

SIMPLICITY AND NATURALNESS IN VOICE PRODUCTION. A Plea and an Argument. By EDWIN WAREHAM. Crown 8vo, cloth, 2/6.

OBSERVATIONS ON THE FLORID SONG. Or Sentiments on the Ancient and Modern Singers. By P. F. TOSI. Translated by Mr. Galliard. With folding Music Examples. 184 pages. A Reprint of this Celebrated Book, first published in 1743. Crown 8vo, boards, with vellum-like back. 21/–.

Recommended to all students of the Italian method of singing by the late Charles Lunn.

"The aged teacher embodies his own experience and that of his contemporaries at a time when the art was probably more thoroughly taught than it has ever been since."—*Grove's Dictionary*.

ELEMENTARY LESSONS ON SIGHT SINGING. Combining the Staff and Tonic Sol-fa Notations. With Music Examples throughout. By J. W. ROSSINGTON, *L.R.A.M.* Cloth, 3/6; paper, 2/–.

For many singers there is only one method of becoming good sight-readers, viz., combining the tonic sol-fa with the staff notation.

THE ART OF VOCAL EXPRESSION. A Popular Handbook for Speakers, Singers, Teachers and Elocutionists. By the REV. CHAS. GIB. Crown 8vo, cloth, 5/–; paper, 2/6.

THE THROAT IN ITS RELATION TO SINGING. By WHITFIELD WARD, *A.M., M.D.* Illustrations. Crown 8vo, cloth, 5/–.

CONTENTS: Anatomical Structure of the Throat; What we See with the Laryngoscope; How we Sing; How we Breathe; How to take Care of the Voice; Hints to Voice Builders; How the Voice is Destroyed; Common Throat Affections of Singers, together with their Treatment, etc.

HOW TO ATTAIN THE SINGING VOICE, or Singing Shorn of its Mysteries. A Popular Handbook for those desirous of winning Success as Singers. By A. RICHARDS BROAD. Crown 8vo, boards, 6/–.

This is the book which fitted Eva Turner to achieve for her wonderful successes in the operatic world (in Italy, Germany, Portugal, etc., as well as in her own country). It should help you to achieve great things too.

TWENTY LESSONS ON THE DEVELOPMENT OF THE VOICE. For Singers, Speakers and Teachers. By G. E. THORP. Crown 8vo, limp cloth, 2/6.

TWELVE LESSONS ON BREATHING AND BREATH CONTROL for Singers, Speakers and Teachers. By GEORGE E. THORP. Crown 8vo, paper covers, 3/–.

TREATISE ON THE TRAINING OF BOYS' VOICES. With Examples and Exercises and Chapters on Choir-Organization. Compiled for the Use of Choirmasters. By GEORGE T. FLEMING. Second Edition. Crown 8vo, cloth, 5/–; paper, 2/6.

THE CENTRAL POINT IN BEAUTIFUL VOICE PRODUCTION. By H. TRAVERS ADAMS, *M.A.* Cloth, 2/6.

HOW TO MANAGE A CHORAL SOCIETY. By N. KILBURN, *Mus.Bac.* Third Edition Revised. Crown 8vo, paper, 1/–.

A CHAT WITH CHORAL SINGERS. By H. W. SPARROW, *A.R.C.O.* 8vo, paper cover, 1/–.

CONTENTS: Reading Music—Tone Production—Breathing—Phrasing—Expression—Enunciation—Blend of Voices—Tone, Attack, Release—Care of the Voice—Suggestions.

HOW TO SING AN ENGLISH BALLAD. By E. PHILP. Eighth Edition. Crown 8vo, paper, 1/–.

50 MUSICAL HINTS TO CLERGYMEN. Management of Breath, Classification of Male Voices, Management of the Voice, The Service. With Twenty specially written Exercises. By GEO. F. GROVER. Cr. 8vo, paper, 1/–.

Printed by DIEMER & REYNOLDS LTD., EASTCOTTS ROAD, BEDFORD